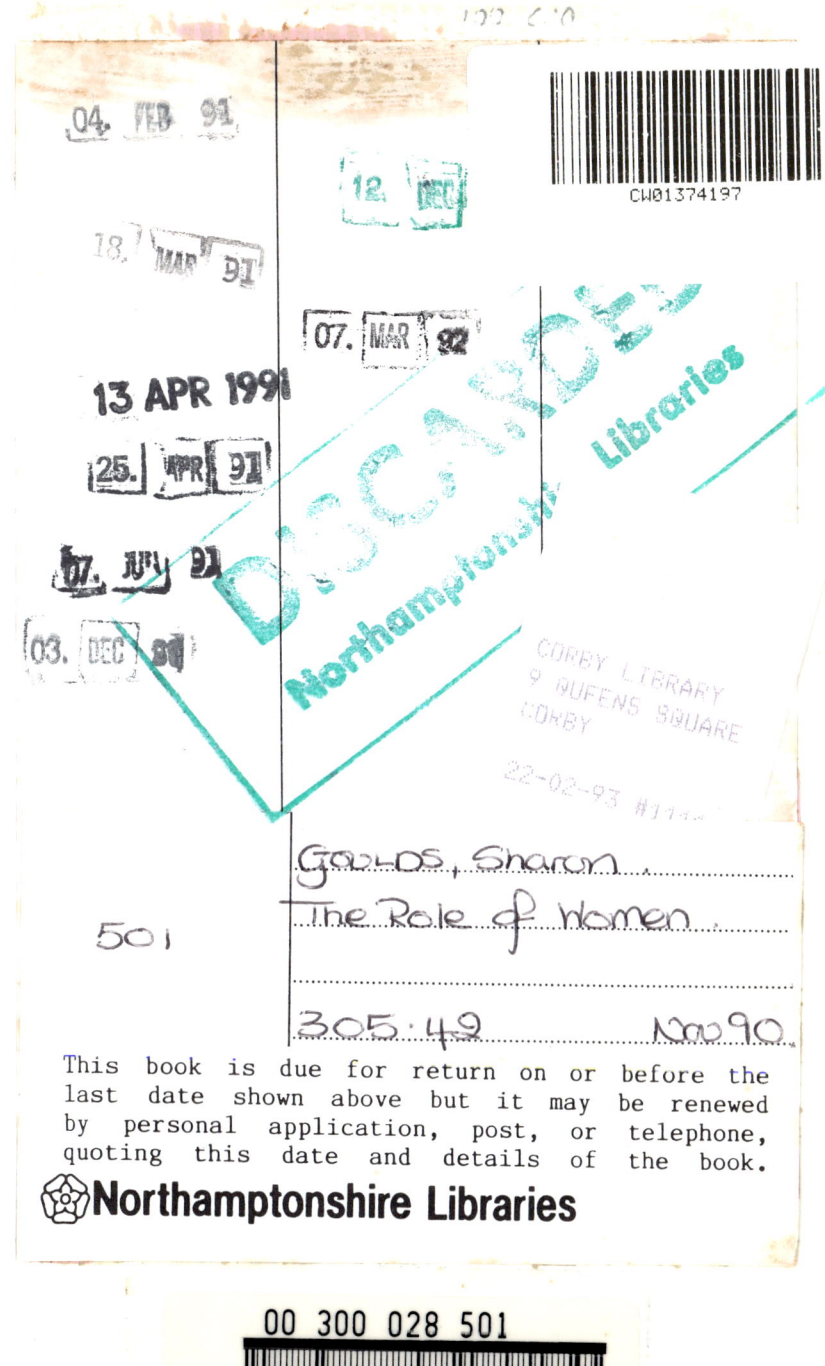

04. FEB 91
18. MAR 91
13 APR 1991
25. APR 91
07. JUL 91
03. DEC 91

12.
07. MAR 92

**DISCARDED**
Northamptonshire Libraries

CORBY LIBRARY
9 QUEENS SQUARE
CORBY
22-02-93

CW01374197

501

Godlos, Sharon
The Role of Women

305.49    No 90

This book is due for return on or before the last date shown above but it may be renewed by personal application, post, or telephone, quoting this date and details of the book.

**Northamptonshire Libraries**

00 300 028 501

*Sharon Goulds*

# The Role of Women

Macdonald

A MACDONALD BOOK

First published in 1985 by
Macdonald & Co. (Publishers) Ltd
London and Sydney

© Sharon Goulds 1985

ISBN 0 356 11018 4

Macdonald & Co. (Publishers) Ltd
Maxwell House
74 Worship Street
London EC2A 2EN

A BPCC PLC company

Printed by Purnell & Sons (Book Production) Ltd
Paulton, near Bristol, Avon

All rights reserved

BRITISH LIBRARY
CATALOGUING IN PUBLICATION DATA

Goulds, Sharon
　　The role of women. – (Debates series)
　　1. Women – Social conditions – Juvenile
　　literature
　　I. Title　II. Series
　　305.4′2　HQ1154

ISBN 0-356-11018-4

# Contents

| | | | |
|---|---|---|---|
| 4 | Women in history | 38 | Happy families? |
| 6 | What is a woman? | 40 | Who does best out of marriage? |
| 8 | What little girls are made of | 42 | Why does marriage survive? |
| 10 | Learning to be a woman | 44 | Are the divorce laws fair? |
| 12 | Have women changed? | 46 | 'Nice girls don't…'? |
| 14 | Should women go out to work? | 48 | The gentle sex? |
| 16 | Housework for all? | 50 | Are women too emotional? |
| 18 | Better off at home? | 52 | Who is more vain? |
| 20 | Jobs for the girls? | 54 | Why do women live longer? |
| 22 | Women can't be managers? | 56 | Equal but different? |
| 24 | Men make natural rulers? | | *Reference* |
| 26 | Why aren't women creative? | 58 | The fight for equality |
| 28 | Education – wasted on girls? | 60 | How to find out more |
| 30 | Are girls less intelligent? | 61 | Reading list |
| 32 | Supporting a wife and family? | 62 | Film and video |
| 34 | Money isn't everything? | 63 | Index |
| 36 | Do women make the best mothers? | 64 | Credits |

# Women

Through the centuries different societies have treated women in different ways. Their social status and the opportunities open to them, though generally inferior to men's, have seen some surprising changes.

> 'Never beat a woman, not even with a flower.'
> *Prophet Mohammed, founder of Islam*

**The ancient world** In Babylonia, in the third century BC, women had considerable scope for financial independence, and were employed as scribes, diviners, hairdressers, shopkeepers, cooks, spinners and weavers. Women in early Egypt, on the other hand, were virtually equal in law to men, but there were few ways in which they could earn a living.

An Egyptian wife could divorce her husband. But a Hebrew wife would be stoned to death for infidelity. Women in Athens during the same period were subject to the absolute authority of their male next-of-kin and rarely went out unchaperoned.

Many societies have practised female infanticide. It was practised by the Romans until the fourth century AD, and resulted in a shortage of suitable wives. It left women, particularly from upper-class families, in a position of relative power.

**Women in medieval times** Women in Moslem society were given property and inheritance rights by Mohammed in the seventh century AD, some way ahead of their European sisters. Moslem men, however, were, and still are, allowed four wives; and in a court of law it took the testimony of two women to equal that of one man.

Christian societies tended to see women in the role of Eve, responsible for mankind's departure from Paradise. The Italian poet Petrarch (1304-74) wrote: 'Woman...is a real devil, an enemy of peace, a source of provocation, a cause of disputes, from whom a man must hold himself apart.'

In feudal Europe, the Lord of the Manor was entitled to the 'droit de seigneur' – a wedding night with a new bride before her husband.

Later, the cult of Mary (mother of Jesus) developed, and was accompanied by a more chivalrous attitude towards women. 'The Lady' became a symbol of virtue, and it became fashionable, at least in courtly society, to put women on a pedestal, considering them pure and incapable of wrong.

Despite this new Age of Chivalry, however, in the fourteenth century the Italians developed the chastity belt, a painful device designed to keep women inviolate while their husbands were away.

*A medieval woman accepts a love token from her courtly knight. In the Middle Ages, the cult of 'the Lady' inspired an idealized view of women which bore little relation to real life.*

# in history

**Women in Asia** In India in the Middle Ages, it was customary for a widow to be burnt to death on her husband's funeral pyre, a custom that continued to some extent into the twentieth century.

In China for more than 2,000 years, women were subject to Confucius's three obediences: 'Obedience to the father and the elder brothers when young, obedience to the husband when married, and obedience to the sons when widowed.' Women also had their feet bound from childhood – tiny feet were considered an attribute, but the result was that most women could scarcely walk.

**Today?** In many societies the bride's family still pays a dowry – land, livestock or money is given to the new husband and his family at the time of the wedding. In family terms, therefore, daughters are more expensive than sons, and daughters-in-law a better economic proposition.

It is still unusual for titles and land to be handed down in the female line. Sons automatically take precedence over daughters, and many families will keep on producing children until they get a son and heir.

Even today, in the western world of women's liberation and equal opportunities, women and men may still be a long way from considering each other of equal value; and there may be many traps for the unwary – as you will discover in this book.

*'I'm afraid it's a girl. Would you prefer to inform your husband yourself?'*
Liv Ullmann in Changing, 1978

Women with their feet bound – an eloquent reminder of the cruelty of this old custom, photographed at a home for the elderly in Peking. Footbinding is now banned in China.

# What is

The dictionary defines a woman as an adult human female. This adult human female takes many forms. We have numerous different images of women and some of these are contradictory.

**Advertising images** If you look at advertisements the pictures presented are very varied. There is woman as Mum providing hearty breakfasts and white shirts, woman as housewife obsessed with the qualities of washing powders and polishes, and woman as sex symbol, pouting over a box of chocolates, pampering herself with bath oils, or flirting on a foreign beach.

> 'Women are there for the children, the kitchen and the church.'
> *German proverb*

A woman, it would seem, can be mysterious and provocative in her off-duty hours, but down-to-earth, thrifty and dedicated in her role as homemaker. Women are there for men to look up to and for men to look down on. Men often consider themselves the protectors of women, but in daily life it is usually women who look after men.

A woman is encouraged to look pretty and sexy, and to make considerable efforts to achieve this if it does not come naturally. Above all, a woman is seen as someone who needs a man. Much of our advertising is designed to persuade a woman to make herself attractive to men.

Once she becomes a wife and mother, however, the prevailing image changes to someone who is 'nice' – homely and comfortable. The woman no longer sizzles with the sexual attraction which presumably hooked her man in the first place; her energy goes instead into cleaning and nurturing. A wife, according to the adverts, is not glamorous and disturbing, but a cosy comfortable nest-builder.

**Women have babies?** However varied or contradictory the images, the major factor that distinguishes the 'adult human female' is her ability to have babies. This ability affects a woman's role throughout her life. It even affects those women who cannot, or choose not to, have children. They are pitied, or viewed as abnormal, perhaps by themselves as well as by other people.

A woman who decides a job is more important to her than a family is a 'career woman'; a woman who refuses to be a wife may be a 'good-time girl' or even a 'scarlet woman'. Where are the 'scarlet men'? Or the 'career men' for that matter?

**The perfect woman?** The 'perfect woman' is one who combines many varied talents – the nurturing mother, the supportive wife, the sex symbol, and the competent career woman – and who does not show the strain! Most women and their 'adult male partners' settle for much less.

The compromise can be a comfortable one for all parties. How many men would feel

*Wife and mother at breakfast time.*

# a woman?

secure with the perfect woman? How many men can live up to the image of the ideal man – successful in his career, handsome in his appearance, masterful in his relationships, protective to his family and quite invulnerable to fear, grief and other untidy emotions?

**Men and women** What a woman is or should be, what role she should be playing, is usually defined in terms of what a man is and of what role he has. Female is seen frequently as the opposite of male.

But different biological functions in the maintaining of the human race, different physical characteristics, do not necessarily

> 'The value of a woman is three-fifths that of a man.'
> *Old Testament, Leviticus 21: 1-7*

produce two groups of people with consistently opposite emotional and intellectual qualities. The average man may have more physical strength than the average woman, but does it follow that he will have more reasoning power, a natural inclination to lead, and much better control over all his emotional responses?

The most beautiful woman in the world?

# What little girls

# are made of

'Sugar and spice and all things nice...'

'Sugar and spice and all things nice, that's what little girls are made of.' Little boys, on the other hand, are made of 'snips and snails and puppy dogs' tails', and are expected to behave accordingly: 'Now my little brother, he's a typical boy, he's only five and yet the other day he punched me and it nearly killed me' (14-year-old girl).

Our nursery rhymes and fairy tales are full of enterprising, energetic and adventurous boys who defeat giants, restore the family fortune and rescue princesses. The girls are more likely to be waiting for a prince to rescue them and their virtues are those of patience under suffering, compassion, delicacy – and they are nearly all physically beautiful!

Many people feel that these early images have an undue influence on children, so that boys identify with Dick Whittington and Jack of the Beanstalk, and the girls with Cinderella and Sleeping Beauty. Others say that both sexes just identify with whoever they see as the hero or heroine in each story, rather than choosing by sex. Nevertheless, the role models are there.

> 'Boys are more intelligent and everything. Girls always giggle.'
> Schoolgirl, 14 years old

**Tomboys and sissies** These different images of boys and girls continue in the childhood comics and magazines that they read. After the age of about 8 or 9, they even read very different sorts of comics. Boys' comics are much more action-packed, with boys having adventures in weird and wonderful places, successfully overcoming all sorts of daunting obstacles. The world of the girls' comic is a more cosy and familiar one, with the adventures taking place in much tamer surroundings.

At a fairly early age, too, girls and boys start to play with very different toys, and to develop their own ideas about what girls do and what boys do. Here's a 14-year-old schoolgirl talking about her brother: 'He's a very feminine boy. He's gentle and good with children...He likes dressing well and things you would normally associate with girls...I used to say that he was sissyish when he was little.'

Boys who play with dolls and are gentle and quiet are 'sissies'; girls who are boisterous and prefer guns and cars are 'tomboys'. Generally it is considered better to be a 'tomboy' than a 'sissy'. Why is it that people are less worried about girls who act like boys are supposed to, than boys who act like girls are supposed to? Does this happen in later life, too?

**In love with love** In their early teens, or even earlier, girls move on to reading romantic comics which most boys would dismiss as 'soppy'. Boys, on the whole, don't read magazines about love but about football or bikes. Girls, if they take their magazines seriously, are living at a level of romantic fantasy which real boys can never live up to.

Boys may also have their fantasies about the perfect romance or the ideal wife, but they are not encouraged in boys in the same way; they are expected to have sexual fantasies and needs, but not to admit to feelings of love or emotional dependence. The 'girlie' magazines and pin-ups marketed for men have no real female equivalent.

This preoccupation with 'love' seems to be a fundamental difference between the sexes at all ages. Love is the woman's province, work the man's: 'They need love and they need work: and work takes priority over love,' the American sociologist Dr Joyce Brothers explained, in *What Every Woman Should Know About Men*.

# Learning to be

When growing up, boys and girls will be influenced by a number of factors. Some are the result of conscious effort on the part of their parents, teachers and the media, some an unconscious assimilation of what goes on in the world around them.

As one teenager said about sex roles: 'Children learn how they are different from one another by the way their parents and friends talk about them – "what a sweet little girl you have and so pretty…What a rascal of a son you have, always getting into mischief". We learn about men and women from our parents' lives, from school, from books and magazines, and from popular music.

Mothers may not want their daughters to repeat the patterns of their own lives, but find it difficult to provide an alternative: 'I wouldn't want my daughter to get married at 20 and have children at 22. There are other things in life than getting married and having children,' said one typical mother. But in almost every family, girls see their mother doing most of the housework and their father making most of the money. Girls see women looking after babies and men looking after cars. Girls play with dolls and boys with machines.

**Contemporary pressures**

'I want to be Bobby's girl,
That's the most important thing to me.
And if I was Bobby's girl
What a faithful, thankful girl I'd be.'
(*Bobby's Girl*, © Klein and Hoffman, 1962)

Each generation creates its own culture of music, clothes and vocabulary which is distinct from the world of parents and teachers. The styles of each era are different, but the blurring of sexual differentiations which took place with the long-haired men of the 1960s and the 'femininity' of pop stars like Boy George do not represent in either case any radical change in the roles of men and women.

The pop world itself is dominated by male performers and producers, with female consumers keeping it all going. The stars are predominantly male, the fans female. It is by and large girls who immerse themselves in the lives of their pop heroes, and boys who buy guitars and drums and practise in draughty halls.

There is a sense in which pop culture looks as though it is rebellious but actually encourages conformity. It looks sexy and glamorous and romantic, all the things that everyday

*Opposite* Female fans admire David Cassidy.

# a woman

lives, particularly the everyday lives of the older generation, are not. But for the girls at least, it is a world that produces idols to worship rather than goals to be achieved.

Wherever girls look, in films and on television, in magazines and on advertising hoardings, women are portrayed as glamorous; the constant message is that it is more important to be beautiful than bright. Girls learn to enhance their beauty and disguise their intelligence, and it is the pretty girl who is the envy of her contemporaries.

> 'I'm strictly a female female
> Whose future I hope will be
> In the arms of a brave and free male
> Who'll enjoy being a guy
> Having a girl like me.'
> From I Enjoy Being a Girl by Rodgers and Hammerstein, 1950s

# Have women

Since the Second World War ideas about women seem to have changed several times. Different eras have wanted different things from women.

**The angel of the hearth** In the immediate postwar period until the late 1950s, there was a lot of emphasis on the value of home and hearth. Women were viewed as their guardians, and the embodiment of all the homely virtues. There was an obvious psychological reason to want order, security and domesticity after the turmoil of war, and women were seen as the natural homemakers; there was also a natural inclination to produce more babies. 'After the war we were ready to give up work and settle down. Your husband went out to work and you looked after him and had his meal ready when he got home and you never thought of working unless you were hard up,' said one. Women's magazines of the late 1940s and '50s reflect this preoccupation with domesticity.

Women were wanted at home for the more practical reason, also, that they were no longer needed at work. Their jobs were required for the men returning from the war. The nurturing role of women was emphasized, they were mothers developing domestic skills. As the economy expanded, they became shoppers in chief, the spearhead of the new consumer boom.

Sheila Rowbotham, a pioneer in the field of women's history, described the '50s as 'an era of elaborate hairdos, constraining clothes and Dr Spock'.

**Sex, drugs and rock and roll** In the 1960s the emphasis changed; an expanding economy meant more jobs and more money, and a greater sense of freedom. The hallmark of the times was not so much home and hearth, as sex, drugs and rock and roll. One magazine

# changed?

*Far left* A 1950s housewife.
*Left* Ten years later – the swinging '60s.

reported in 1966: 'Women are being encouraged from all sides to have more sex.' For many, the availability of the pill took away the fear of pregnancy.

It was an era that released women from the role of domestic angel only to replace it with the image of the liberated woman who had to be sexy, independent and self-confident. The '60s saw the rebirth of the Women's Liberation Movement and the beginnings of a new campaign for equal rights and equal opportunities.

**The party's over** The 1970s saw some consolidation of women's rights with equal pay and sex discrimination legislation, but the worsening economic climate again had its effect on the role of women.

> 'In the next 30 years, housewives as mothers have vital work to do in ensuring adequate continuance of the British race and of British ideals in the world.'
> *Beveridge Report, 1942*

Unemployment now is forcing women back to the home to free jobs for men. Between 1975 and 1980, official unemployment among women in Britain trebled, compared to a fifty per cent rise among men. Cuts in social services keep women at home to care not only for their children but also for the elderly. One male industrialist said: 'It is a time when women must be prepared to make sacrifices.' In most western economies, recession is taking its toll on women's employment first. The women of the '80s may look different from the women of the '40s, but their situation, and society's attitude to them, is not much changed.

# Should women

For many people a woman's prime role is that of homemaker. Once she is married a woman is expected to put home and family first. A man is supposed to look after his wife and family by working outside the home, the woman by working within it. In fact 30 per cent of women with children under four work some hours outside the home, and by the time the youngest child is ten, this figure has risen to 70 per cent.

It is frequently taken for granted that women are working for pin money only, just to help out and supply some of life's luxuries; single women are only 'marking time' until they marry. Women are said to have jobs, but not careers, while women who do go out to work are sometimes loudly criticised.

**Working mothers neglect their children?** Working mothers are often accused of neglecting their children. It is said that children whose mothers go out to work will feel less secure than those whose mothers stay at home. Increases in juvenile crime and vandalism are often blamed on maternal neglect.

However, a recent study of the children of working mothers indicates that they are no more or less likely to be delinquents or vandals than any other group of children. The father's behaviour may be just as significant in encouraging delinquent behaviour. 'We've been talking to boys who have been classed as delinquents about their home life and one thing that does show up is that in general their fathers are the sort who do a lot of drinking, going to the betting shop and don't work' (a youth worker quoted in *Kitchen Sink or Swim* by Deirdre Sanders and Jane Read).

A mother with a career and other interests outside the home may be helping her children to independence, and developing their curiosity about life in a way that may be beneficial rather than disturbing.

What certainly does affect women and children, however, is the availability or lack of childcare facilities. In Britain, state facilities for small children are worse than in many other developed countries, and nowadays there is rarely an extended family network that can step in and help.

In countries such as the USSR, where state childcare support is provided, many more women do go out to work. But Russian women share with women in many western societies a concern about the adequacy of the care that is provided. In 1980, American women complained to a presidential committee that not only were there not enough childcare facilities, but where they did exist, 'the teacher-pupil ratio was very poor, many institutions were unclean and the equipment limited'.

**Taking jobs from men?** In times of high unemployment there is another objection to women working – they take men's jobs. 'If married women did not work,' some say, 'there would be no unemployment.' There is talk of a 'family wage' so that each household has one salary, and the situation is avoided where some households have two wage earners and some none.

It used to be quite common for a woman to be obliged to give up her job when she married. Until 1944 women teachers had to stop work on marriage. Nowadays it is more likely to be on the birth of her first child that a woman gives up paid employment. Why do we exclude women from the right to work so readily?

> 'A huge proportion of the nation's human resources – over half the population's – remain untapped in most areas of public and economic life.'
> Equal Opportunities Commission, 1984

# go out to work?

**The male breadwinner?** Many families, particularly working-class ones, have always found two wages necessary to keep the household going. Losing either wage has a profound effect on the family budget.

Although women employed in the public sector are particularly vulnerable to cuts affecting their jobs, in some areas traditional 'women's work' has survived the depression of the '80s better than the heavier industrial jobs usually reserved for men. Women have sometimes become the main breadwinners – though in other cases they have been expected to step aside to let men take over the jobs that are available.

Women themselves often see the man as the main breadwinner, and are uneasy if they are at work while he is at home looking after the house and the children. One explained: 'I don't agree with the wife going out to work and the husband staying at home and looking after the kids. I'd rather stay at home all day if it was that way.'

Some husbands actively discourage their wives from going out to work, considering it a slur on their ability to support the family.

> 'If the good Lord had intended us all having equal rights to go out to work, he wouldn't have created man and woman.'
> *Patrick Jenkin, MP, 1979*

American women at work – down the mines.

# Housework

Housework is definitely considered women's work. A man may help with it, but even in families where both parties have jobs, the primary responsibility for the home usually rests with the woman. A recent magazine survey revealed that 90 per cent of all housework is still done by women.

Things have not changed much: 'A man's job in those days was not in the house; they came home at six and that was the end of it. I never saw my father do a thing in the house and I never saw him go shopping,' said a housewife, born in 1901.

**Wages and housework** One of the disadvantages of housework as a job is that it is a solitary occupation, with none of the social compensations that people get from even the most repetitive tasks outside the home. Other disadvantages include the unsocial hours (you never clock off), and the fact that you don't normally get paid for it. You get your board and lodging and some housekeeping money which enables you to do the job, but no money which you quite simply earn, that enables you to go out for a drink, a meal, or buy yourself a record or clothes, or even give the kids a treat.

Should there be wages, then, for housework? A few years ago, a large insurance company worked out that a housewife was worth £204 a week: 'As such, she is worth about as much as a bishop, a sergeant major or a town's fire chief.'

**Men and housework** Men often have specific jobs at home – they may bring in the coal, clean shoes or fit shelves and other DIY jobs. Traditionally they change plugs and maintain and clean cars. They may also cook one particular meal each week. In families where there is a big weekly supermarket shopping

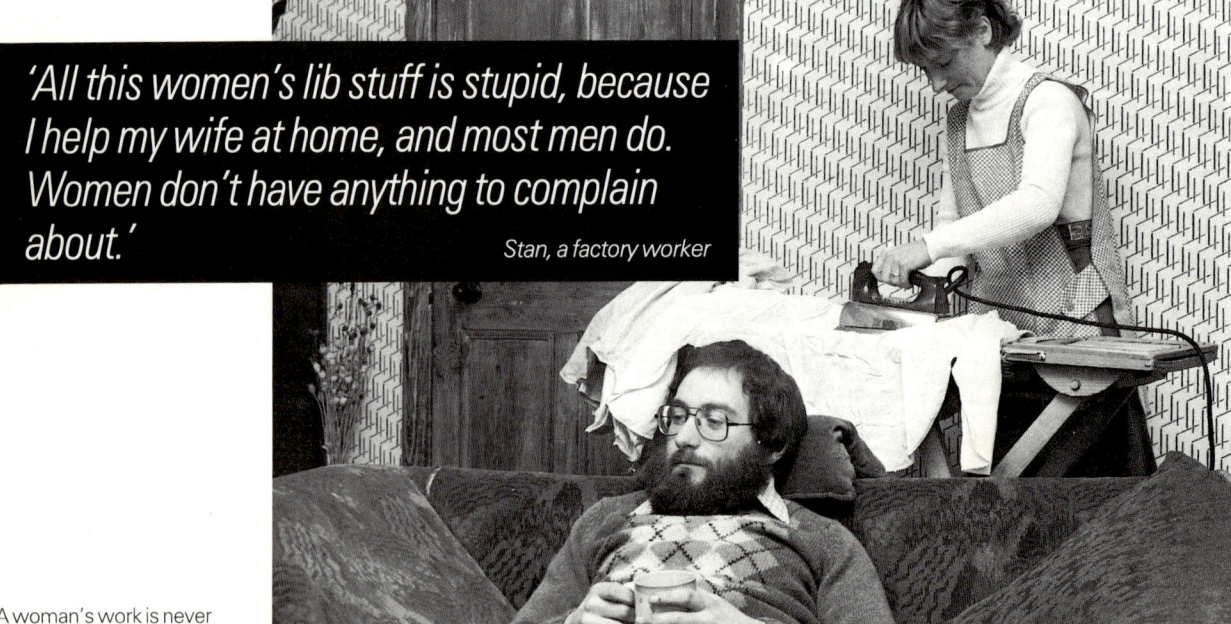

'All this women's lib stuff is stupid, because I help my wife at home, and most men do. Women don't have anything to complain about.'

*Stan, a factory worker*

'A woman's work is never done.'

# for all?

they may help there, if only at the end to help carry the bags.

Most men do not hoover, dust, polish, change sheets, wash clothes, iron, wash dishes, cook meals, dress the children, deliver or collect the children from school, take time off when they are sick, or look after elderly relatives. Most would feel very insulted if asked to – these jobs are just not masculine.

Women, too, often find they will ask their daughters to help around the house, but do not think of asking their sons. Only recently has the assumption been challenged that girls do cookery at school and boys do woodwork.

If the woman of the house is sick or away, it is frequently assumed that the man is incapable of looking after himself; other female members of the family will rally round and cook, wash and iron for him. Some men resent this expectation of incompetence, others take advantage of it.

In the same way, women may pride themselves on their competence as housewives. They can tell themselves they are better at it than men, that it's quicker to do it yourself than ask him to help: 'He says I'm too fussy. I'll go over it again anyway. So he won't bother,' said one. Other women resent the assumption that they will do it, especially if they are working outside the home as well. You can take pride in a polished floor, a well-ironed shirt, a clean bath, but unfortunately these tasks are repetitive and tend to get taken for granted.

So do family meals. Functional home cooking is a chore usually performed by women, while 'chefs' are frequently men. Is it not strange that cooking as a profession is male-dominated, when in most homes it is women who do the cooking?

Ten per cent of the housework is done by men.

# Better off

**M**iddle-class women with a good education and the chance of some job satisfaction may well consider it important to have a career, but for most women the prospect of getting married and not having to work represents a welcome escape from very boring jobs. 'Anything's better than working here. Well, most women get married, don't they? Not all of them work all their lives like a man. Put it this way, I don't want to work when I'm married' (Val, a factory worker).

One of the perceived advantages of being a woman is the ability to opt out of going to work, if only for a few years. 'I don't want to be a boy because they have horrible jobs to do for 50 years,' said one teenager. Being at home and looking after children is considered preferable to most of the jobs available. Housework at least seems to offer the freedom to be your own boss and organize your own day.

> 'I do think that some women use marriage as a retreat, as a way of avoiding responsibility for their own lives.' *Woman quoted in a magazine article*

Another reason why women may not want to work after marriage is their awareness of the double load they would have to carry. 'I don't want to work full time. You work all day and then you've got to go home and work – well, it's too much really' (Val, a factory worker).

**Is housework enough?** A lot of women may be anxious to give up work and become wives and mothers, seeing housework as a more pleasant option; but there are also plenty of wives and mothers anxious to be working, and not just for the money. One magazine survey found that four out of five women would still want to go out to work even in an ideal world, with all financial pressure removed.

Women get bored and lonely at home and need a break from the children. If nothing else, work provides company. Pearl, a factory worker, explained: 'Well, I've enjoyed every minute. More friends. When you're home like that, you're lonely.' Work, however menial, also confers a status, a justification for existence.

Some women feel that they vegetate at home. 'I feel working is important. I'm sure otherwise I'd become very boring,' said one. Work provides a topic of conversation, a

# at home?

relief from talking to and about children.

In a survey of housewives conducted by the sociologist Ann Oakley, 70 per cent were dissatisfied with the role of the housewife, and three-quarters found it monotonous. Generally, housework was compared unfavourable with work outside the home which at least offered company, better status and financial reward.

Very many girls at school continue to see their future in terms of being wives and mothers. According to one 15-year-old schoolgirl, careers are something that men have: 'I think it suits men really. Once men start out on something they go ahead, but women always change their minds, and never do good in full-time careers, really.'

Girls are acutely aware of the problems of combining childcare with paid work, but they are no less aware, these days, of the desirability of not becoming totally dependent on their husbands. As one said, 'Apart from the extra money, if anything went wrong with the marriage she would have to support herself, fall back on her job.' Whether you view housework as slave labour or a cushy option, there is no guarantee that a housewife has a job for life.

Happy in their work – women from a Sunderland shipyard.

# Jobs for

In many countries it is now illegal for employers to discriminate against people on the grounds of their sex; despite this, most employment still falls into jobs that are recognizably women's, and those that are men's. Women are nurses, secretaries, receptionists, teachers, telephonists, clerks, cleaners and factory workers. Girls rarely do apprenticeships, and there are very few female electricians, plumbers or bricklayers.

Women are often excluded from certain jobs because they are said to be physically not strong enough. Yet in the Second World War women took on a lot of heavy industrial work, working on the line in car and munitions factories. In the nineteenth century British women and children went down the mines, and American women do so today, working alongside men. In 1943 there was a woman president of the TUC, and in 1946 women were admitted to the diplomatic service. Yet, despite the fact that women had driven buses in the First World War, it was not until 1974 that London Transport was able to persuade the unions to accept women bus drivers.

**Equal pay?** Female employees are concentrated in low-paid occupations. Service industries like education, health, catering, and local and national government account for over 50 per cent of all women employees. Factories frequently employ women in areas where there are no men doing 'broadly similar work'. Women work in the lowest grades, doing repetitive tasks at the bottom of the payscale. 'I can't imagine a man doing my work. It's too boring for a man' (quoted in *Girls, Wives, Factory Lives* by Anna Pollert).

Despite legislation, women's salaries generally remain lower than men's. Many women feel that if employers did pay women the same wages as men, 'they'll just put men into our jobs'; or, as one male factory worker

Snow clearers in Moscow.

# the girls?

put it, 'when it comes to equal pay, an employer, if he's got any sense at all, will pick a man.'

Employers often believe that women have more time off because they or the children are ill, though there is no evidence to support this. Others prefer to employ women because they see them as more conscientious than men, and less status-conscious. A man will expect more secretarial back-up, for example, and more perks. In some industries he may also be considered more militant.

Women are sometimes accused of lacking the necessary authority for certain jobs. However, women who have worked their way up the promotion ladder so as to be even considered for top jobs are likely to be better than most of the male applicants.

**That's a man's job?** Girls are often encouraged to aim for certain jobs or professions; girls who might have been engineers are guided into the secretarial field. Girls themselves often think they wouldn't be good as technicians, economists or doctors, but would feel comfortable as bank clerks or nurses. 'I would like to know about openings in industry. Engineering interests me, but I think it's probably a man's job. It's dirty,' said one schoolgirl.

In the USA, a policy of positive discrimination (which means that women are favoured because they are women) has made some inroads into 'men's' jobs. It certainly makes it easier for the next generation of female applicants to get a job since there is proof that women can do it. Positive discrimination is sometimes criticised because it may promote a woman over a better male candidate and may in fact promote somebody above their ability. Used properly it ensures women in general a fair chance in areas of employment from which prejudice has excluded them. The only way that prejudice will be eradicated is to have women there actually doing traditional men's work. Logically there would seem to be few areas that women could not tackle.

**The obligatory 'dolly'** Some women get employed, not as much through positive discrimination as through the philosophy of the statutory woman. 'Equality' has become fashionable, and one woman may be promoted in order to disarm criticism – without making any fundamental change. To be this statutory female can place a great strain on the woman concerned, and many may avoid putting themselves up for promotion because of it.

> 'If a firm has any sense, they wouldn't train a woman for a responsible job.'
> — Male chargehand

A Danish woman priest.

# Women can't be managers?

If women do have the same qualities of leadership as men, why are there so few of them in positions of authority?

In virtually all fields, women bosses are in short supply. Even in areas like the health services where women workers predominate, those at the top of the tree, the consultants and the hospital administrators, are nearly always men. The female membership of professional bodies ranging from law and banking through to chemical engineering remains disproportionately low. There are few women in positions of authority in trade unions either.

> *'I wouldn't want to work for a woman.'*
> *Female secretary*

Women often have to be encouraged to put themselves up for office. Sometimes this is the result of lack of confidence, but it can also be the difficulty of taking on responsibility outside the home. It is often more awkward for a woman to get away to an evening meeting, or to bring work home. 'At night you just can't manage. You've got to get home, and do the housework and cook meals; you just don't feel up to anything else' (Pearl, a factory worker).

**Getting to the top** The same may apply to a woman seeking promotion; with other demands on her time and energy, a woman may not want to take on extra responsibility at work. A survey in France in 1982 found that working women still spent an average of four hours a day on domestic duties, compared to a man's one hour 40 minutes. Four hours on top of a day's work leaves little energy for other responsibilities.

Some say that women do not have the same drive to succeed as men; or is it perhaps that they need a lot more drive in order to succeed? Between 1911 and 1971, the percentage of women who became bosses rose from 18 per cent to only 24 per cent. This may be because the years during which men are pushing on with their careers – the mid 20s to the mid 30s – are also the years when most women have their children. No matter how quickly a woman gets back to work, it is easy to fall behind in the promotion race, especially if you have more than one child. Children may also change a woman's priorities in a way they don't a man's.

**It's a man's world?** Another factor may be that men in authority will promote other men because they find them easier to work with. They view other men as 'natural' management material. Women, too, often prefer to work for a male boss rather than a female one.

Women who do display qualities of leadership are often described as 'masculine' – and if a woman is described in these terms it is more likely to be a criticism than a compliment.

It may also be more of a strain for a woman to be a boss. It is easy to overreact, to see chauvinism where none exists or in fact to be the victim of it from both male and female colleagues. A woman may often have to be more assertive than a man in a similar position in order to be able to do her job successfully. This in turn can antagonize her male colleagues and encourage them to close ranks against her.

*Opposite* A woman executive in a French car company. Why are there not more women in her position?

'I don't see why you don't have female executives – just because their body's a bit different, it doesn't matter.' *Schoolgirl, 15 years old*

# Men make

So far the twentieth century has only produced four major female political leaders: Golda Meir (Israel), Indira Gandhi (India), Sirimavo Bandaranaike (Sri Lanka) and Margaret Thatcher (UK). Many people, men and women, feel uncomfortable about a woman ruler. Politicians themselves cannot decide whether having women in prominent and powerful positions loses or gains them votes.

Although women form 52 per cent of the world's population, there is no parliament in the world where 52 per cent of the members are women. Are women discriminated against in the political world? Do we want leaders who are decisive, authoritarian and powerful, warriors to lead us into war? And are these seen as 'masculine' rather than 'feminine' qualities? 'Margaret Thatcher is leader of the Conservative Party because she is the best man we've got,' said a Conservative MP in 1979.

**Is it lack of interest?** Even when major efforts are made to get women into politics at both local and national level, they seldom come forward in large enough numbers to improve the present imbalance. Women's traditional family responsibilities are probably largely responsible for their failure to put themselves forward. In most countries, particularly at national level, political life is not compatible with family life.

It is possible that women do not feel confident enough to enter the political arena. The ability to express opinions forcibly or to speak out in public and expect to be listened to are not traits generally encouraged in women. Even the women who are successful in politics tend to get office in the education and social services departments, the 'soft' options, rather than defence or finance, or even foreign policy, which are seen as male territory.

In Britain since 1945, women have only provided about 4 per cent of elected politicians, and in France, Canada and the USA the proportion of women is only 2 per cent. In most countries women are under-represented in national politics. In Sweden and Finland, where the proportion of women is comparatively high, they still only account for 22 per cent of elected politicians. There is no evidence to suggest that voters show any disfavour to women candidates. The prejudice is more likely to be in the minds of those who select candidates within the traditional political parties.

**Women in politics** Women's political activity has more frequently been attached to specific campaigns. The beginning of this

Women in politics, supporting nuclear disarmament.

# natural rulers?

century saw women all over the developed world campaigning for the right to vote. In France, it was not until 1944 that women got the vote.

At present women are conspicuous for their involvement with the peace movement. There is a woman at the head of CND, and women protesting at Greenham Common. The leader of the German 'Green' party, Petra Kelly, is also a woman.

Women have also run campaigns around issues that are seen as specifically 'female' - abortion, maternity allowances, childcare provisions and even divorce.

Do women enter the political world in this way, joining pressure groups, building an alternative political perspective, because that is the way they choose to be involved, or because that is the only way they are permitted to be involved? Do women not run for the world's parliaments because they are not interested in the hierarchical career politics represented by the House of Commons, the Bundestag and the Senate?

> 'Seeing Margaret Thatcher at conferences with all those men – well, it doesn't look right, does it?'
> *South Wales housewife*

Britain's first woman Prime Minister. At this dinner for US President Reagan, there is not another woman in sight.

# Why aren't women

There is no female Shakespeare, Goethe or Picasso. The creative fields – both arts and sciences – are dominated by men.

It may be true that the talents of some women artists and writers have been overlooked by a male-oriented society. There are examples of women whose talents have been ignored, but this alone does not account for the discrepancy. Most people, if asked to name artists, film directors, journalists, poets, sculptors, photographers or cartoonists, would automatically name a man; even if asked specifically for a woman, many people would not be able to think of one.

The one area where women have been more successful is in writing novels. Some of the famous novelists of the nineteenth century, however, the Brontë sisters, George

Making music: the Lydia D'Ustebyn Swing Orchestra.

# creative?

Sand and George Eliot, felt obliged to use male pseudonyms in order not only to get published but to protect themselves against the accusation of dealing with 'unladylike' subjects. The nineteenth and twentieth centuries abound with women novelists – George Eliot and Jane Austen are as well known as Dickens and Thackeray, Doris Lessing as famous as Anthony Burgess; Barbara Cartland and Agatha Christie sell as well as Frederick Forsyth and Raymond Chandler, and are probably better known by the general public.

In the last 15 years there has been a general revival of interest in women writers. Several new publishing houses which concentrate on women writers have come into being (see page 62). Not only have they encouraged new writers but they have also reissued almost forgotten work, revitalizing the female literary tradition and firmly establishing women's creativity in this field. These new publishing lists include writers from all over the world.

**Domestic boundaries** The differences between male and female novelists may also indicate something of a more general difference between the sexes. Women are often criticised for the small scope of their work – they concentrate on the personal, the settings are often domestic, and the story provided by personal relationships rather than the wide sweep of human affairs.

Women are writing about what they know – their lives are often bounded by domesticity and they are frequently excluded from the wider scene. Men may be concerned with war or politics. Women may be the victims of either, but otherwise are traditionally excluded.

The domestic and personal concerns that women reveal when they do create may also indicate why they create less. It is more difficult for a woman to abandon the small tasks of daily life, to expect someone else to get on with them and allow herself the space in which to paint, write, take photographs or compose music. Men are certainly better at being singleminded – that sort of determination is admired and encouraged in them. Women more frequently just feel plain selfish.

**Where are the women scientists?** In the field of science women are even less noticeable. Even in medicine, one of the first scientific careers open to women, women on the whole still become nurses rather than doctors. Women are directed towards the 'caring' side of medicine, and away from the more prestigious academic work. 'Caring' is seen, perhaps, as suitably feminine.

*'Women are better at dull, repetitive jobs.'*
Office of Population Survey, 1975

Few of the world's scientific breakthroughs can be credited to a woman. Again, this does not necessarily mean that women are simply less brainy, or less talented. They are often just worse educated. In most European countries, education for women has dragged behind education for men. Men have been going to university since the Middle Ages. In Britain women were not allowed to take degrees until the 1890s. Girls' schools used to be notoriously bad at sciences, and often did not have any facilities.

In many countries co-education still does not mean that expectations of what is suitable for boys and girls, or what they are capable of, are equal.

# Education –

**B**oys and girls may go to the same school, share the same classrooms and teachers, but do they get the same education? Research done in primary schools indicates that boys and girls are treated differently right from the start, and that five-year-olds' ideas of male and female roles are already fairly rigidly fixed. One survey discovered that boys in particular had very firm ideas of what girls could do – and, more important perhaps, what they could not do.

**Do girls get stupider as they get older?** Girls do very well when they first go to school, learning to read, write, add and subtract at least as quickly as boys. In the first few years, they often do better than boys. Small girls may be naturally brighter and quicker than small boys, but evidence also suggests that what they in fact do is to work harder and concentrate more. Again this could be because girls are expected to be 'good', encouraged to be more passive and obedient than boys – who are encouraged to be 'boys', mischievous, energetic and cheeky.

At school, girls keep up with boys until the age of 15 or 16. Exam results at this stage are fairly equal, but from then on boys tend to do better academically than girls.

Boys are expected to be good at and interested in science, girls in arts. This imbalance is particularly marked in Britain where the education system encourages specialization at an earlier age than in many other countries.

**She'll only get married?** Do people stop encouraging girls beyond a certain stage because 'it's not worth it, she'll only get married'? Or do girls themselves give up and concentrate on being attractive to boys?

Even if you accept the idea that a man will go out to work and keep a woman and children, is it sensible to assume that bringing up children is so unimportant that it can safely be left to the least educated among us? The nineteenth-century feminist, Mary Wollstonecraft, wrote: 'To be a good mother, a woman must have sense and that independence of mind which few possess who are taught to depend entirely on their husbands.'

> *'A learned or even over-accomplished woman is one of the most intolerable monsters in creation.'*
> Dr Hodgson, nineteenth-century educationalist

Girls are often now admitted to the same courses at school as boys, and vice versa, but it is still unusual for girls to apply to study carpentry, motor mechanics or technical drawing, or for boys to be queuing up to tackle needlework or cookery. In Britain, for example, in 1977, for every boy who passed 'O' level cookery, there were 61 girls; for every girl who passed 'O' level woodwork, there were 166 boys. 'Only a couple of people did physics – I don't remember ever having the chance. You hardly ever found anyone doing it for exams…But we really hated needlework and cookery,' said one girl, talking about her convent school education.

People's ideas of what is suitable for boys and girls, for men and women, seem to lag behind the laws that make things possible. Is there a real demand for change, or has all this legislation been foisted on the average person at school or at work by a few militant activists?

# wasted on girls?

Sharing lessons in a London school.

# Are girls

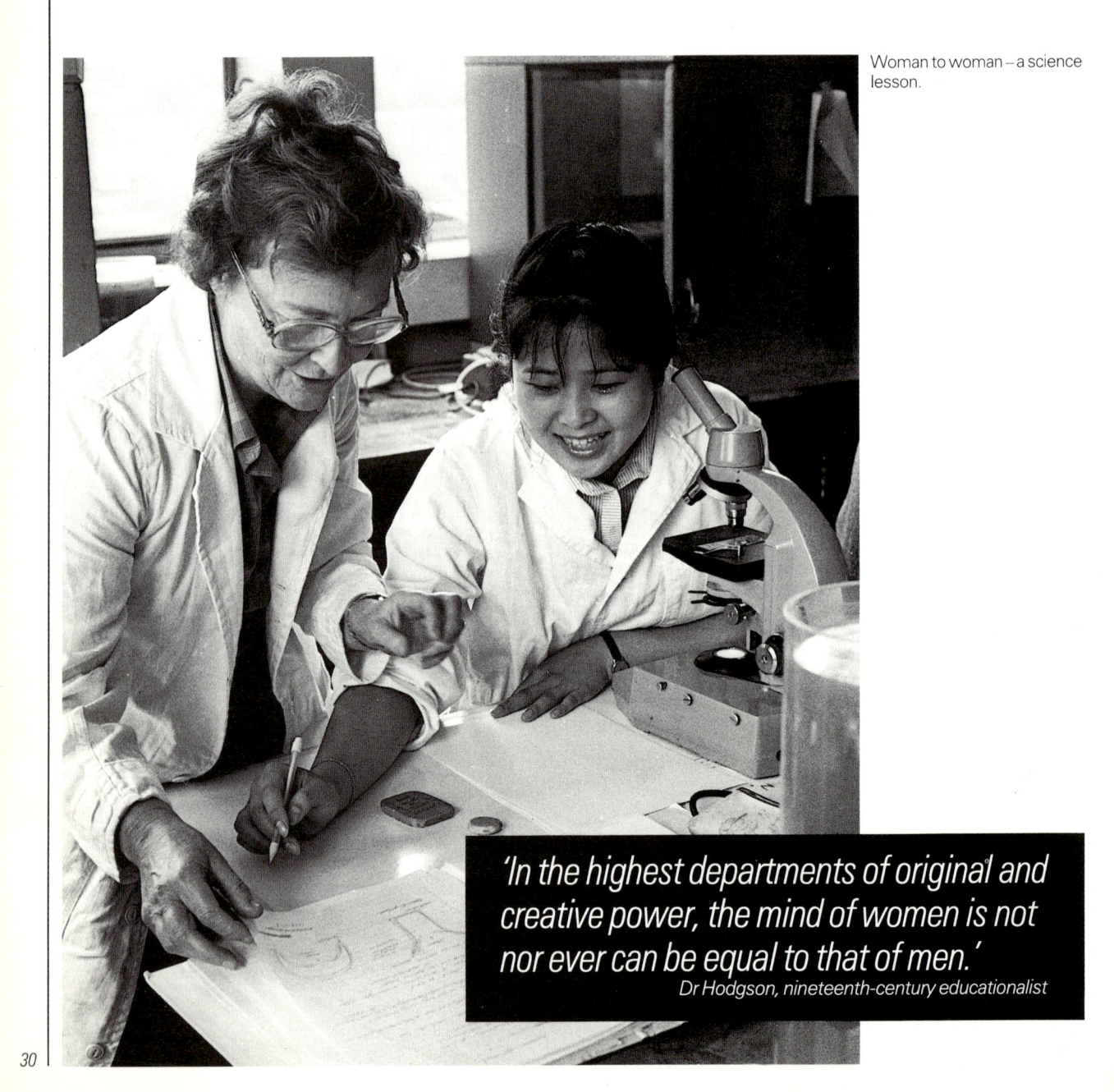

Woman to woman – a science lesson.

'In the highest departments of original and creative power, the mind of women is not nor ever can be equal to that of men.'
*Dr Hodgson, nineteenth-century educationalist*

30

# less intelligent?

If you compare the figures of boys and girls going to university, girls come out badly, gaining on average less than 40 per cent of university places. In some subjects, however, there are more women than men undergraduates; languages, arts and education often have more than 50 per cent women students, while engineering and technology have less than 10 per cent. Is this because women's brains are more adapted to subjects like literature and sociology? Is it somehow feminine to read French, speak German and be interested in poetry and the theatre, while learning about computers, microchips and engines is masculine?

**Men need jobs?** The courses that men do at university and college are often more directly related to work, to the whole business of getting a job, while 'women's' subjects are somehow less practical. Is this difference a reflection of the fact that society still does not really expect a woman to have to earn a living, or not for very long anyhow, or does it in fact measure a very real difference between male and female abilities? 'Most women enter business with their ambitions fixed on achieving independence in a kitchen as some lucky man's wife, while most men start with the desire to do well enough to provide the kitchen,' said one business manager.

If electronics is masculine and literature feminine, what happens to subjects like law and architecture, psychology and medicine? Just over 20 per cent of architectural students are women and just over 40 per cent of medical students. These subjects may not sound as oppressively masculine as chemical engineering or veterinary science, but doctors and architects are still predominantly men.

**Women need encouragement?** Should girls get more careers advice at schools than boys? Do they need more encouragement because they are inclined themselves to give up and get sidetracked where boys will persevere with what they really want to do? One mother, a factory worker, explained: 'You should encourage girls in school now – then there'll come a time when they'll want to do something and they'll be able to. I don't want my Shirley to be stuck in a factory.'

The statement from the Equal Opportunities Commission that Britain is 'failing to develop the potential skills and talents of half its population simply because they are girls' is echoed in a report from New Zealand: 'We cannot afford to waste half our potential labour force – the brains and talents of New Zealand women.'

That female talents are being ignored seems to be borne out by the experience of girls themselves: 'I was interested in engineering, but was advised against it because of the competition there would be from boys,' explained one.

**Do boys like clever girls?** The pressure to conform is also a factor. Are girls reluctant to be seen as 'brainy'? Do they prefer not to compete with boys because they begin to see 'success' in terms of having boyfriends? Do they think boys mind if their girlfriend is more academic than them, has better exam results?

Statistics show that girls do better academically at single-sex schools. Is this because in mixed schools teachers concentrate their attention on the boys; because girls work harder when there are no boys around; or because, in a single-sex school, girls do not mind getting a reputation for being clever?

# Supporting a wife

Men in general earn more money than women. Nevertheless, in many homes, the men's wages are insufficient to support a family, and over the last two decades, women's contribution to the family income has increased dramatically.

In the late 1970s 50 per cent of married women were working outside the home, and many of those not working were in a sense 'between jobs' – taking some time off while they had their children. Even among women with very young children, substantial numbers (21 per cent in Britain) had paid employment. The percentage is even higher in other European countries. In France 43 per cent of women with children under 3 work, in West Germany 32 per cent and in East Germany as many as 80 per cent. In Australia 40 per cent of mothers with children under 5 are working.

Many families do not have a male breadwinner at all. In Canada in 1981, over 11 per cent of all families were single-parent families; 83 per cent of these were headed by women. This pattern is repeated in most western societies.

**A family man?** The image of the 'family', a male breadwinner supporting a wife and two children, is obviously a false one, but both men and women feel obliged to live up to it. Many men hate the idea of their wives having to work, and even today some actively oppose it. Many (perhaps even most) men would feel particularly humiliated if they were actually supported by a woman.

Many women, too, feel it is much more important for a man to have a job. 'Well, don't you think that a man needs a job more? I think a married man needs a job more than a woman,' said one. This is not just because a man can earn more or because they don't want him 'under my feet all day', but also an acknowledgement of the psychological impact that being unable to support his wife and family can have on a man, brought up to see that as his role in life, proof of his masculinity.

The construction of the traditional family may be unfair to both men and women. A man may resent his hard-earned money being swallowed up by the wife and kids, and feel trapped in a job he really dislikes by his financial responsibilities. 'You know when you're 30, with a wife and a couple of kids in tow, the things you can do are quite limited really,' explained a male factory worker. A man can see his wife's role at home as a cushy job, and resent her apparent freedom and lack of responsibilities.

A woman may feel like an unpaid drudge with little responsibility, or stimulus, outside the home. She may resent doing paid work outside the house because she does not get any corresponding help with work inside it. 'When you think you've got to go home and start all over again…Some nights I don't sit down till 9 o'clock,' said one.

**Head of the household?** Women are often seen as the centre of family life. They keep the family together, that is their first job. A man, however, often gets the title of 'head of the household'. Even today, businesses will address themselves to the head of the household, as will surveys and government depart-

> '*A wife and her children must belong to the husband as an apple tree and its fruit belong to the gardener.*'
> Napoleon Bonaparte

# and family?

ments. In France, the notion of a head of the family, inherited from the Code Napoleon, was abolished in 1970 by government act.

Man's role as the family boss is emphasized by the fact that, in many cultures, a woman takes the man's surname. Even when women do keep their own names, or when both surnames are used, children tend to take their father's name.

Are men in fact masters in their own homes, or do they just think they are because women let them? Or is the whole concept of the 'head' of the family just an outdated idea that has lingered on in official jargon?

The family portrait. Is this where our image of family life comes from?

# Money isn't

**M**oney, or the lack of it, has a very real effect on our lives. We all know that money isn't everything and many people claim that it isn't important to them; but our lives are still ruled by the need to earn it and to pay our way. Statistically most marital rows, including violent rows, are to do with money – or the lack of it.

**Who pays the piper calls the tune?** On a global scale women are the poor relations: 'Women constitute half the world's population, perform nearly two-thirds of its work hours, receive one-tenth of the world's income and own one-hundredth of the world's property' (UN figures).

Even in countries where equal pay legislation has been enforced for some time, women in full-time employment earn considerably less than men. In Canada, the Equal Pay Act came into force in 1956; but by 1980 women, because they are concentrated in low paid jobs, only earned 58.8 per cent of what men earned.

Many women earn very little or no money at all. In many cases a woman may be totally

Women traders in a Ghana street market. The market is run by women.

# everything?

dependent on a man's earnings. No matter how much she 'earns her keep' within the home, her lack of financial independence is bound to keep her in a subordinate role in the relationship. 'If you're too dependent on one person, the husband, it is very tempting for the husband to make the wife more the slave,' noted one schoolgirl.

**Money and the state** In Britain, when a woman does earn, her earnings are automatically treated as part of her husband's for tax purposes – unless they especially ask to be taxed separately. If a woman gets a tax rebate it is sent to her husband, unless he asks for it to be sent to her. In the USA, couples can elect each year whether to be taxed together or separately, and if they are taxed separately they have no further involvement in each other's tax affairs. Couples are also taxed separately in New Zealand, but in Australia they have no choice but to be taxed as a unit.

The British tax system automatically awards a tax allowance to married men, and a married woman cannot claim supplementary benefit from the state because her husband is expected to support her. There are cases where single women have had benefit stopped because a man has stayed the night. It seems to be assumed, as far as the state is concerned, that where there is a man involved, he will be responsible for the woman financially.

**Holding the purse strings** Couples have different ways of dealing with money. One recent survey showed that three-quarters of husbands did not tell their wives what they earned; at the other end of the scale is the man who hands over his entire wage packet to his wife and just gets back some pocket money.

*'It's a great life, having someone to keep you.'*
Margaret, a housewife

Women are usually in charge of the housekeeping, but may feel that they have to ask specially for money to spend on themselves. In other cases husbands complain that their wives have the run of a joint bank account and no compunction about using it. For such women, being financially dependent would seem to be a privilege rather than a problem!

# Do women make

The 'maternal touch' – Pete feeds Joe.

'I do believe that women with young children have a primary duty to be at home to look after them.'

Sir Nicholas Bonsor, MP

# the best mothers?

Looking after children is definitely considered by most people as women's work. A recent magazine survey showed that, even in families where the mother worked full-time, three-quarters of the fathers had never taken time off when the children were ill, and one in three had never even read to their own children. Somehow cuddling and playing with babies and young children is not seen as masculine, though rough and tumble and games with older ones may be.

**Fathers make good mothers, too** Does a woman become a 'mother' because she has a baby? Or is it the close contact involved in caring for the child that makes her 'maternal'? Many now believe that it is only practice that makes women good at childcare. It would seem that men who are in close contact with babies, who change nappies and make up bottles, become just as expert as women, and just as affectionate. Once a child is born, he or she can easily be 'mothered' by a man.

Some men are inhibited from expressing their affection for their children physically because they see the cuddles and the verbal nonsense as somehow sissy. Some absolutely refuse even to be seen pushing a pram. Yet they may be missing out on one of life's real pleasures, which is no more feminine than it is masculine.

**Do babies need mothers?** Not all women like babies, and even those that do, do not necessarily want to spend all their time with one.

Some childcare experts have said that the mother is the proper person to be at home looking after her child, at least for the first five years. Others believe that it is actually bad for the child to have such concentrated care from one person, and that babies and young children benefit from more stimulus, more varied company and less loaded attention. It

> *'Motherliness is a complex quality not confined to women and not present in all mothers.'*
> Dr Ann Dally, sociologist

is certainly not clear that the sex of the person who looks after the child is of crucial importance. It could just as well be a man as a woman.

**Watching your children grow** A woman who has carried a baby for nine months and then breastfed it for several more months may take responsibility for the child so naturally that she unconsciously excludes the father from the relationship.

Many fathers are excluded from their families for much of their working lives. Work patterns frequently mean that they see little of the children, and most men would not dream of asking for time off to take a child to the dentist or to see a school play. In some families a father is just an authority figure to threaten the children with: 'You wait till your father gets home'. Once the children have grown up, many men feel acutely aware of what they have missed.

At the moment, with rising unemployment, many men are spending more time at home. Some find it hard to adapt: 'It would be a lot easier if men had always been brought up to be involved with the family,' said one. Others have adapted to housework and children, like Harry, an unemployed labourer: 'I enjoy doing things around the house...If I got a job, I'd still want to be involved with the house and children. I'm a lot closer to them now.'

In the book *Kitchen Sink or Swim*, Chips Oakley described his feelings: 'There is something delightful about watching your baby grow up rather than come home at night and be told.'

# Happy

The family exists and endures presumably because it is seen as a convenient way of bringing up children. Despite the pressures of being the breadwinner, the family set-up is also fairly convenient and comfortable for men. Most men get their washing done, their meals cooked, some help with the household bills – and tax relief.

It is women who take the stresses of family life: the double load of working inside and outside the home, and the responsibility for the children and the elderly. It is by and large women who head single-parent families, and single women who stay at home to look after elderly parents.

We grow up with the image of a happy family: the parents, forever in love, bringing up two healthy, happy babies; but the reality is more fraught. Parents fight and babies get battered. Most people who have looked after young children alone full-time can understand how that happens. Interestingly, 83 per cent of the children on the NSPCC's 'at risk' file have mothers at home full-time, compared with only 49 per cent in society generally. The nuclear family would seem not so much a recipe for living happily ever after as a 'psychological and emotional pressure cooker', as one writer described it.

**Other solutions** Other societies organize their lives in different ways. Even in cultures where the family is the norm, it may not be the standard nuclear family of husband, wife and two children, but a much larger extended family which includes grandparents, uncles, aunts and cousins, all living together or near enough to provide real help with the children, with illness, and with day-to-day living.

Israel developed the kibbutz system. Groups of people live communally, and the children are automatically looked after in

*'I know it's old-fashioned, but I see it as a labour of love.'* Quoted in Now We Are 30 by Mary Ingham

A family party at Christmas – a traditional happy scene?

# families?

nurseries. In some kibbutz the children even sleep away from their parents, in dormitories.

In socialist countries the state sometimes plays a more active part in what we call 'family life'. Nursery facilities are automatically provided for pre-school children, and housing is organized to provide some communal facilities such as laundries and canteens.

Communal living may not suit everybody, and state help can seem too much like dictatorship, but the effect of providing some back-up for families is not to destroy family life but to enhance it. Particularly for women, it allows more choice and more control over their own lives.

**Families need fathers** The way that family life is organized effectively means that fathers seldom play much part in it. While the children are small they are working their hardest, either to further their career or just to put in enough overtime to keep the family going.

Better childcare facilities and better paid work for women should mean that men would not lose out on their children, nor have to work so hard at frequently unrewarding jobs. Brian, a single parent, explained: 'I think men should compromise a bit. A lot of my mates think more of their pay packets than of their families. They take their wives for granted. It's home for dinner and then down to the pub. I now think that fathers should spend as much time with their children as mothers do.'

'When poverty comes through the door, love flies out the window.' *Traditional*

A different sort of family — children on an Israeli kibbutz. But kibbutz life also has its pressures.

# Who does best

Despite the rising divorce rate, marriage is no less popular than it was 100 years ago. One in four marriages ends in divorce, but the remarriage rate is also high, particularly among men; the remarriage rate for divorced men is between three and four times as high as it is for divorced women.

This would seem to indicate that men are more enthusiastic about being married than all those wife and mother-in-law jokes would lead one to expect. However, the main reason for the difference is more likely to be the fact that is is somehow more acceptable for a man to marry a much younger woman than vice versa. This means that middle-aged men have a greater choice of partners than middle-aged women.

However it is also true that many more women than men say their marriages are unhappy, and that many married women suffer from stress. Women's experience of marriage then, would seem to be less favourable than men's, which may make them reluctant to take the plunge a second time.

> 'A wife's duty is promoting the happiness of others, to make sacrifices so that his enjoyment may be enhanced.'
> Mrs Beeton, Book of Household Management

**Do women expect too much from marriage?** Are women disappointed in marriage because they expect more out of it than men? This could be because women invest a lot of themselves in a marriage and do not get as much back, whereas men spread their investment in other areas of their lives. As the poet Byron wrote:

'Man's love is of man's life a thing apart,
'Tis women's whole existence.'

We are brought up with a very romantic image of perfect love that no real-life relationship can ever sustain. It may also be true that men are not educated to provide emotionally what women are encouraged to expect from marriage.

Women are not taught to inhibit their emotions. They tend to grow up more used to intimate situations, and conversations about their more private thoughts, feelings and insecurities, where a man may be embarrassed even with his wife. Men have not often had the chance to practise this sort of relationship. 'Men and women need the same things, but women are more aware of what's needed. Men take it all for granted,' said a young wife, quoted in a magazine article.

# out of marriage?

**Should married couples be faithful to each other?** In the West marriage is traditionally monogamous, and adultery is usually still grounds for divorce. Men's infidelity, however, is more likely to be tolerated by society, and by their wives. Certainly, in terms of opportunity and expense, a man is better placed to get away with it. A 'roving eye' is seen as part of a man's nature, whereas a wife's infidelity would have a more shattering effect on marriage.

A man is expected to be a 'bit of a lad', and this could help a wife to feel less humiliated by her husband's infidelity; she would be able, perhaps, to take it less personally because after all 'men are like that'. Society's expectations of male and female do not supply a man with the same escape if his wife is unfaithful. Also a wife's infidelity may affect the paternity of the children.

**On the shelf?** Single women may do better at work than married women (the opposite is true for men) and suffer less from nervous tension, but there is still a stigma attached to being a 'spinster'. A single woman is considered by some a failure, while a single man is somehow a victor. A bachelor who has 'escaped' is the envy of his friends, and an unmarried man is never 'left on the shelf'.

A Jewish wedding. Most cultures mark a 'marriage' with some solemnity.

# Why does marriage

Why didn't marriage go out of the window with the sexual liberation of the 1960s? What happened to all that brave talk about not needing legal sanctions: 'We don't need no piece of paper from the city hall keeping us tight and true,' as Joni Mitchell sang?

**For better, for worse?** Marriage as an institution survives despite a 25 per cent failure rate. Does it survive because people like to make a public statement of their love for one another? Does the public commitment help them through the bad patches?

Or is there a more practical reason for marriage? Is it encouraged because it is an efficient economic unit, an easy way of maintaining whatever workforce is necessary to keep the country going? A woman will bring up the next generation of workers, sustain the present one and always be there as a reserve labour force in times of crisis. Are people exploited by marriage or supported by it – or a bit of both?

**Arranged marriages** Some societies treat marriage in a much more businesslike way. The marriage is a partnership arranged by the families. 'Your parents don't just give you away to another person, he is very carefully chosen. You can't choose someone of your own,' explained an Asian schoolgirl, living in London. The couple do not 'fall in love' before marriage; they may hardly even know each other. The marriage is seen primarily as a way of continuing the family, making the man an efficient worker and providing economic support for the woman.

Divorce rates among arranged marriages are low, but this does not necessarily indicate that it is a successful way to treat marriage. It is more likely that, in societies where marriages are arranged, divorce is quite unacceptable as a solution for unhappiness.

Possibly couples whose marriages are arranged have a less romantic idea of marriage, and may not invest all their emotional energy into this one relationship. Certainly the family is more likely to be there to extend support, and provide other close associations which may take some of the weight from the married couple. They are not expected to be everything to each other.

**Marriage and unemployment** For previous generations getting married was the only way to leave home. Now young people share flats or bedsits with each other, and can even 'live in sin' without too much social disapproval, if they can afford it.

The unemployment of the 1980s may have had an effect on the patterns of young marriage and parenthood. The generation that grew up in the '60s, under the influence of a reborn women's liberation movement and a flourishing economy offering more opportunities to both men and women, did not plunge so quickly into marriage and babies.

Nowadays, with little work around, getting

*Right* Young people today – still the marrying kind.

*Below* Will the marriage work? The astrologer/priest checks on this Hindu couple's compatability before their wedding.

# survive?

married or becoming parents may appear to be one of few ways that young people can mark their entry into adult life. Even if lack of money forces them to live in the parental home, being married and parents themselves may help them to seem more grown up. Is marriage still popular today partly because of the status it conveys?

> 'Marriage is popular because it combines the maximum of temptation with the maximum of opportunity.'
> *George Bernard Shaw in* Man and Superman

> 'Marriage? I don't believe in it. It's just a piece of paper.'
> *René, a factory worker*

# Are the divorce

If present trends continue, one in three couples getting married will eventually split up. Since divorce became easier in the late 1960s, the new laws have been much criticised. Some people think that divorce is now too easy; in Britain, for example, you can get divorced after two years with mutual consent; after five years one partner can divorce another against his or her will.

This ruling was labelled the Casanova charter; it was seen primarily as enabling middle-aged men to divorce their middle-aged wives and marry younger women. It made a mockery of any idea of 'Till death us do part'. Wives who had supported their husbands through the early years to achieve some measure of comfort and financial security found themselves replaced just when life began to look easier.

**A meal ticket for life?** At the moment, though, it is men not women who are trying to change the divorce laws – because of alimony. This is the money men are ordered to pay to support their ex-wives and children. Men do not see themselves as benefiting from a Casanova's charter, but as being saddled with having to support 'alimony drones' for the rest of their lives.

> 'Girls can no longer be brought up believing in the myth of happily ever after... none of us can be certain of that any more.'
> Quoted in Now We Are 30 by Mary Ingham

Most incomes hardly stretch to one family let alone two, and alimony payments can make life very hard for the second family. At the same time, the children of a first marriage clearly should expect some support from their father; and a wife who has put all her efforts into supporting a husband's career, and at the very least needs retraining in order to get a job, may be justified in demanding some financial compensation for those years. It is much harder in most cases for a woman to support a family on her own because women's wages are generally lower than men's.

Often the law tries to take this into consideration by 'putting the parties in the same financial position as they would have been had the marriage not broken down' – their joint earnings are divided between them. Pressure from men's groups in the USA has had some success in eliminating the concept of alimony, in favour of a system of child support which ceases once the children reach a certain age.

In Britain the wife is legally entitled to only one-third of any matrimonial property. In many of the American states, on the other hand, married couples own property in common, and in the event of divorce it is split on a 50/50 basis.

Divorce puts a financial burden on everybody. The man feels he has two families to support, and the ex-wife still has in most cases to manage on less money than before. Many husbands particularly resent paying maintenance if the wife has been the 'guilty partner' or initiated the divorce in the first place. Maintenance agreements at the moment do not always take conduct into account. Should they? Or should the question of why the marriage broke down be kept separate from its financial consequences?

**What happens to the children?** A man may be expected to support his ex-wife and children, but he is rarely able to live with his children. After divorce most fathers are deprived of a normal family relationship with their kids: custody is almost automatically awarded to the mother.

This may reflect the reality of the situation. The mother will probably have spent more

# laws fair?

time looking after the children, and living with her may generally be less emotionally disruptive for them. However, the emotional damage this may do to the father is usually ignored or underestimated. Should children be asked whom they want to live with? Or would any such choice just make life more difficult for them?

**Second time around?** Whatever financial and emotional strain a divorce may put on a man, his chances of living 'happily ever after' with someone else are nearly four times greater than his wife's.

Access for Dad – taking the children out at the weekend is not the same as being with them all week.

# 'Nice girls

*Opposite* Would it be different if...?

*Waiting to be asked to dance.*

Sex before marriage has generally become more acceptable, but there are still differences in people's attitudes towards the sexual activity of men and women.

Parents tend to be stricter and more protective towards their daughters than their sons. A boy who is sexually active 'is a bit of a lad', a girl is 'a bit of a slag'. The double standard is not just operated by the older generation. One schoolgirl explained: 'It's funny really 'cause when you go out with a bloke, they expect you to give them a bit ...but when they want to get married, they want a girl who's a virgin, yet they've just taken some other girl's virginity – so she can't marry a bloke who wants her to be a virgin. It's daft, it really is!'

It's also only comparatively recently that women have been expected to enjoy rather than endure sex: 'And then when I slowly began to get the feeling that it was really alright and I got carried away and started doing things to him and enjoying it, I used to apologize afterwards. And he said to me..."Look don't be stupid. I mean women don't just lie there"' (quoted in *Dutiful Daughters* by Jean McCrindle and Sheila Rowbotham).

**Do men want just one thing?** 'Men are ashamed of their own sensitivity to suffering and love because they have been taught to regard these as feminine. They are afraid of being feminine because that means other men will despise them,' wrote Sheila Rowbotham, a pioneer in the field of women's history.

Is there, then, a fundamental difference between women's attitudes to sex and men's? Is it true that women want an emotional experience and men a physical one? A survey that asked teenagers what qualities they valued in a person of the other sex did find that boys concentrated much more on physical appearances (a good figure was consistently high on their list), whereas girls were generally more interested in having someone to talk to. A boy's status among his friends is enhanced by a reputation for sexual experience.

And here, again, men are expected to take the initiative. It is still the custom for a girl or a woman to be asked out. The man makes the first advances and he will probably pay for at least the first date. Why can't a girl ask a boy out? It might be fairer and easier all round if these roles were shared out. The girl would not have to wait anxiously for the 'phone to ring, and the boy would not have the constant worry of being turned down.

# don't...'?

It is obviously not seen as feminine for a girl or woman to make romantic or sexual advances, and this is probably tied up with the whole business of reputation – if a woman makes a move, she may be labelled as promiscuous or aggressive. Are men and boys given the choice, perhaps, because later it is they who will be considered to have the main responsibility for keeping a woman and possibly children?

**'I'm pregnant'** It is likely that the attitudes towards male and female sexual activity are so different because of the simple fact that a girl can get pregnant. The baby would be seen primarily as her responsibility and that of her family. She would have to make the decision about having the baby or having an abortion, keeping the baby or having it adopted.

If a woman has had more than one sexual partner concurrently, she may not even know who the child's father is. Traditionally the issue of paternity was one reason why women were expected to be more chaste than men.

If a boy does 'get a girl in trouble', should they automatically get married? Would the boy be criticised for leaving the girl in the lurch if he did not offer marriage?

**Are men and women incompatible?** 'At the moment men and women are not being brought up to be able to live with each other,' wrote Maureen Green in *The Sunday Times*. Girls want someone to talk to, and boys want someone who looks good. Boys are expected to be randy all the time, girls to restrain themselves and the boys. Men's sexual activity is at its height in their late teens, while women are supposed to be most sexually responsive in their 30s. However, society frowns upon older women going out with younger men. What keeps the whole thing going?

**Would you be more careful if it was you that got pregnant?**

Contraception is one of the facts of life. Anyone, married or single, can get free advice on contraception from their doctor or family planning clinic. You can find your local clinic under Family Planning in the telephone directory or Yellow Pages.

'What all women have to face is that every man wants the woman he marries to be pure and untouched by other men.'

Barbara Cartland, romantic novelist

# The gentle

Women have a reputation for being nice, for being gentle, kind and unselfish. Is this reputation justified? Is it something that men prefer to believe of women ('most men like to think of women as gentle, intuitive, swayed by pleasant emotions,' said the journalist Bel Mooney)? Or have women conned men into accepting this image of themselves for their own devious purposes?

Certainly men commit more violent crime than women; 93 per cent of murders are committed by men, and 92 per cent of crimes involving drunkenness. Yet women are more likely to be convicted of cruelty to children. Similarly the women warders in Nazi concentration camps did not distinguish themselves by their kindness and were often accused of being more vicious than the men.

Do women generally repress their nastiness more than men because they are expected to, though in an environment where unpleasantness is expected from them they can turn just as nasty? If a woman wants something, is she more inclined to use charm where a man might favour force or more aggressive tactics?

woman. Women have also been combatants in various South American liberation struggles, and amongst the Vietcong.

If women really want equality, perhaps they should be prepared to take their share of the less pleasant jobs such as warfare – though some would say that, if women did have real influence on the way the world was run, wars would be much less frequent.

> 'They don't like girls to swear, goodness knows why.'
> *Schoolgirl talking about boys*

**Should women fight?** In our culture, women do not join the armed forces to fight but only to support the men who are fighting. You do not often find an armed policewoman, and even in the Israeli army, where women are supposed to play a more equal role, they do not send women to the front line.

In the twentieth century, women have become more conspicuous in unconventional warfare. Women have hijacked planes for the Palestinians, and one of the leaders of the Baader-Meinhof group (who used violence to further their political ends) was a

# sex?

**The protective male?** Do men like the idea of women being gentle so that they can feel protective and strong? Small chivalrous gestures like opening doors, or giving up a seat on a bus, may make both the man and the woman feel good. It seems contradictory, though, that it is often this same traditional man, who gives up his seat to a stranger, who will get home and expect his wife, girlfriend, mother or sister to wait on him hand and foot.

Most women do not need looking after. Physically they have considerably more endurance than men. Women survive starvation, exposure, fatigue and hunger much better than men do. Why is it, then, that it is men who conquer Everest, explore the Antarctic, and expose themselves to the dangers of mountaineering and deep-sea diving?

...Pointing a gun...Holding the baby...

# Are women

It is usually taken for granted that men are the rational ones and women are emotional: 'Women, then, are only children of a larger growth; they have an entertaining tattle and sometimes wit; but for solid reasoning and good sense, I never knew in my life one that had it,' wrote the essayist Lord Chesterfield in 1774.

There is, however, a contradiction in the idea of women as the children to be indulged; in the 1950s Dr Eustace Chesser of the Society for Sex Education and Guidance was urging women to believe that 'there is a great deal of the child in a man, and a wife should in a sense be a mother to her husband as well as her child'.

> 'When they're upset girls can cry and let it out, but a boy keeps it inside him and makes it worse.'
> Schoolgirl, quoted in 'Just Like a Girl' by Sue Sharpe

**Men can't be emotional?** Being emotional is clearly something that women value. They are not ashamed of their own emotional reactions. A survey among schoolgirls found that, to many of them, the ability to cry over books and films and generally let their emotions out was one of the positive aspects of being a girl.

Men are taught to keep a stiff upper lip and generally to be embarrassed by emotional displays. They may perhaps release their feelings in more formal ways than women – on the sports field for example; and it is usually only on the football ground that you see physical affection between men. The other way that men sometimes express their feelings is through violence.

Men's embarrassment at emotional displays can be easily exploited, and some

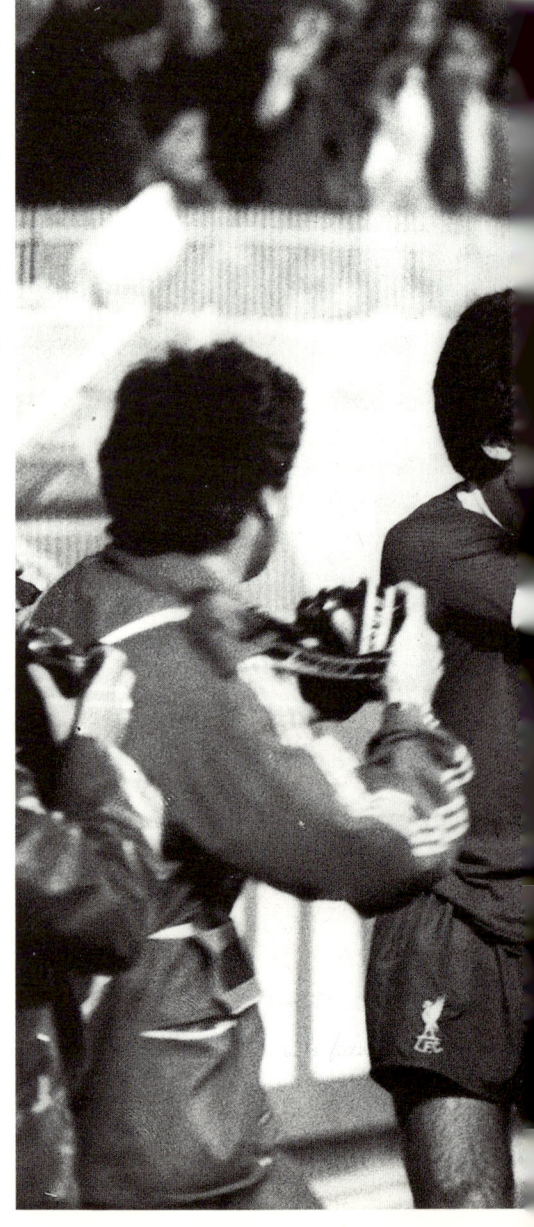

*Right* An emotional outburst during the European Cup.

# too emotional?

women use this, bursting into tears or otherwise creating a scene in order to get their own way. Emotional blackmail, however, is not the prerogative of one sex. Men will sulk and withdraw affection when they want their own way, judging that most women will find this hard to ignore.

Women are supposed to be more sensitive than men, to have more delicate sensibilities, but it is men who baulk at dirty nappies and incontinent grandparents.

**Other cultures** The taboo about male emotion is not common to all cultures. Men from Mediterranean countries are supposed to express their passions a lot more freely than the reserved British, for example; and men from Arab cultures are usually much less inhibited about expressing their affection for each other. Even in Britain, it is only since Victorian times that it has been viewed as so very unmanly to cry, or to express love, fear or apprehension.

Female sensibility, on the other hand, was at its height in the Victorian age; women were expected to swoon at the slightest impropriety. This may have been because middle-class women needed to be seen as particularly sensitive so that men could look after them and feel particularly protective. (Working-class women could not afford the luxury of such displays of 'femininity'.) Unfortunately, however, this type of so-called 'emotion', a fashion like any other, has given genuine emotional response a bad name.

There appears to be no intrinsic reason why men should be rational and women emotional; both seem to get pushed into roles which can only be a strain, and this stereotyping has repercussions not only in people's personal lives but in their choice of jobs and even leisure activities.

# Who is

Keeping up appearances.

Appearance seems to play a much larger part in a woman's life than a man's. It is considered 'feminine' to be interested in clothes and make-up and to worry about hairstyles. It is women by and large who have their faces lifted and their noses reshaped. It is women who traditionally take ages getting ready to go out.

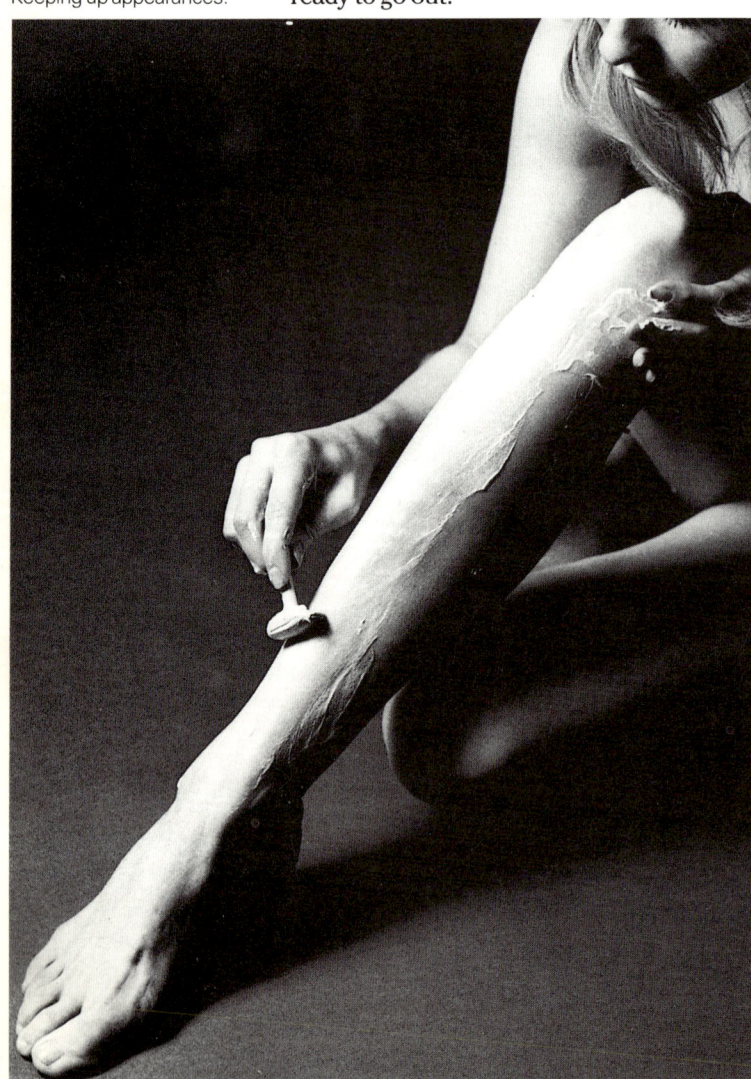

Women worry more about their appearance, but they also get more fun out of fashion and dressing up generally. 'Brighter colours, prettier clothes and a better choice of fashion' were some of the advantages of being a girl offered by a group of 15-year-olds.

It is important for a woman to be pretty or stylish because women are judged far more on their appearance than are men. However, women themselves are far less influenced by male good looks than men are by female; which may suggest that it is mainly men, rather than women, who think looking good is important.

**Dressing up** In previous generations men dressed up just as much as women. In the eighteenth century, for example, men wore powder and paint, wigs and beauty spots, and did not find them at odds with the more obviously masculine activities of duelling, drinking and riding. In the twentieth century young men at different times have gone hippie or punk, worn bright colours and earrings, had their hair streaked or permed – in most cases only to conform later on.

Adolescent boys care as much about their appearance as girls, and spend just as much time and energy cultivating an image. However, a boy's interest in his appearance is not reinforced and is more likely to be discouraged as sissy. A girl, on the other hand, is encouraged to see her appearance as absolutely central to her life; not only will someone only marry her if she looks good, but good looks are considered essential for getting a job. As one advertisement put it: 'I so want this job – but I don't stand a chance with a skin like mine.'

**Pictures of women** Women are continually confronted by pictures of other women. These images from advertising, not just the beautiful and sexy, but also the happy and pleasant-looking housewife or, nowadays,

# more vain?

the competent and dynamic career woman, give women a lot to live up to. They also encourage us all to view women very much in terms of what they look like.

Attractive women sell cars, paint, electrical gadgets, drink and tobacco, as well as the more obvious products like perfume, stockings and make-up. Given this barrage of beauty, it is not surprising that the average woman is caught from time to time looking anxiously in the mirror. Why not use a half-naked man to sell bricks or bath oil, or at least put him on page 3 of the *Sun*?

**Sex symbols** Do women feel flattered if men whistle at them in the street? Are they pleased or embarrassed if a man makes a suggestive remark about their appearance? Is it a compliment or an insult? Do women want to be admired as sexy by all men, only by certain men, or not admired just for their appearance at all?

Boy George making an appearance.

'Keep young and beautiful,
It's your duty to be beautiful,
Keep young and beautiful,
If you want to be loved.'
From Roman Scandals *by Warren and Dubin, 1933*

# Why do women

*Opposite* A woman may outlive her husband by many years.

Statistically, women live considerably longer than men, but have more illnesses and are twice as likely to be mentally ill. Men, it appears, have 'a short life but a merry one'. Men are more likely to die of disease related to 'merriness' – heart or liver disease from too much food and drink, or lung cancer from too many cigarettes. However it is also true that women are turning increasingly to drink and cigarettes, and that the gap between male and female life expectancy is closing.

**Life after work** One of the more obvious differences between male and female life-cycles is that a man's is more clearly divided into sections: school, work, and retirement. His family does not provide the consistent thread it does for most women, whose domestic responsibilities are always with them.

Many men find retirement difficult to cope with; they are at a loss being in the house all day, and they do not have the money to do all the things that they dreamed of doing while at work. Women are more used to being housebound and can always find something to do. They probably progress more easily from mother to grandmother. They find a role within the family at each stage of life, whereas a man can find his role abruptly taken from him.

A lot of apparently healthy and lively men go downhill very quickly when they retire. Once they stop work it is harder for them to keep fit as not even the activity of housework is demanded of them (whereas women always have a reason to be on their feet).

**The middle years** For women, middle age is probably the most traumatic period. Middle-aged men usually have some sort of status in the community and at work, while a middle-aged woman is going through a period when she is least needed by her family: her children are virtually grown-up and there are as yet no grandchildren.

A woman may also feel more vulnerable to wrinkles and grey hair; 'I always used my appearance to get what I wanted' is a technique she feels will no longer work. Depression, and both mental and physical illness increase markedly among women in their 40s and 50s. It is easy to blame all this on the menopause, but the other social and psychological reasons should not be ignored.

'If she takes a career for a few years she can do it after she's had her children. Otherwise, when she's about 35 to 45 she's got nothing,' noted one astute teenager. Work may not be the cure for all ills, but women often find it is better than 'nothing'. It at least gives them something else to think about, people to talk to and something to do: 'She's not a person you put away in a cupboard, someone that cleans the house and has children, and the husband does everything else. No, it's not fair – after all she's living,' said another schoolgirl talking about her mother.

If men and women shared family and work more equally, men might be able to enjoy old age without feeling redundant, and women to avoid the depressions of middle age. They would also have a lot more in common, and that fact alone might make the process of retirement easier, and men might live with it longer.

> 'The whole future frightens me. I think when the children are grown up I'm going to be very lonely.'
> 
> Sally Jordan, housewife

# live longer?

# Equal

Women's fight for equal rights and equal opportunities, one of the most important struggles of the twentieth century, has generally received a hostile reception from men. For the last 100 years, the women's movement has been criticised as ugly, belittled as mad and dismissed as merely sex-starved. 'What they need is a man,' people said. Women campaigning for the vote in the early part of this century were told 'Go home to mind your babies', in much the same way as the women demonstrating today at Greenham Common.

> 'The women who want women's rights Want mostly women's charms.' Punch, 1870

Nevertheless there have been some successes: the vote itself, laws banning sex discrimination or introducing equal pay, fairer divorce laws and less punitive abortion legislation. All this has had to be fought for.

Women's legal status has certainly improved, but what about their position in society? Do men, and women themselves, continue to see women as the 'lesser man'? One schoolgirl said: 'I agree with some of it like equal pay and equal opportunity in jobs, but I like men to be domineering and I don't like women always trying to be better than men.' Is that a commonly held view?

**Are men frightened of women?** According to an article in *Honey* magazine, 'We don't need men to be our providers, our meal tickets. You'd think they'd be grateful but

> 'I think that women's lib is the most stupid thing. How can a man be equal to a woman?' Schoolgirl, quoted in 'Just Like a Girl' by Sue Sharpe

they're not. They think it's a threat to their masculinity.'

A recent opinion survey echoed this, revealing that the men of the 1980s are thoroughly confused about their role: 'They are afraid that women are out to take their jobs and to take over as the family breadwinner. They fear, too, that their wives will end up earning more than they do.' Modern man may feel he has changed with the times, but his wife seldom agrees: any change, she says, has had to be forced upon him by women.

Feminism seems to have become a dirty word. The attitude of most men, and some women, towards it is that 'they're just trying to stir up trouble'. Prime Minister Margaret Thatcher said, 'The battle for woman's rights has been largely won.' Rights may indeed have been won, but is that always the same as liberation?

Women who dismiss the women's movement and say that they are not in any way part of it nevertheless have benefited from its battles. There is not only a change in their rights, but a shift in attitudes. Society in general has become aware of 'sexism'; and in so many ways woman can no longer be automatically discriminated against.

**The way forward?** Most of the action to change the role of women has been directed to giving them an equal chance in a man's world. The next stage, perhaps, should be to give men an equal chance in a woman's world, and to acknowledge the positive value of what is now decried as women's work or dismissed as merely female emotion.

Mary Kenny, a '60s fighter for women's rights, wrote in 1978: 'The next phase of women's liberation is not to have to prove how tough and unassailable you are, but to be unafraid of showing your needs and your vulnerability – not because this is slavishly "feminine" in the helpless sense, but because it's what makes us all human.'

# but different?

'I want to be a bricklayer when I grow up.'

# Reference

## *The fight for equality*

**1792** Mary Wollstonecraft's *Vindication of the Rights of Women* is published arguing the case for women's equality.

**1848** British parliament debates the issue of votes for women for the first time, in response to a petition signed by thousands of women.

**1869** Women in the frontier territory of Wyoming in America are the first to get the vote and the right to serve on juries.

**1893** Women in New Zealand are given the vote.

**1902** Women in Australia get the vote, followed by two European countries, Finland and Norway, in 1906 and 1907.

From 1897, when the National Union of Women's Suffrage Societies is established, to the outbreak of the First World War in 1914, women in Britain campaign strenuously for votes for women.

**1913** As part of the suffrage campaign, Emily Davidson throws herself under the King's horse on Derby Day.

**1914** Outbreak of the First World War.

**1917** Russian Revolution gives the vote to the women of Russia.

**1918** In Britain the Representation of the People Act gives the vote to virtually all men over 21, and all women over 30.

Suffragettes on the march – votes for women, c. 1910.

The end of the First World War in 1918 sees votes for women introduced in Austria, Canada, Czechoslovakia, Germany, the Netherlands, and Poland.

**1919** Nancy Astor becomes Britain's first woman MP to take her seat in the House of Commons. (Constance Markiewicz was the first woman MP elected but, as a member of Sinn Fein, refused to take her seat.)

**1920** Female suffrage becomes part of the American constitution.

**1928** Women in Britain are given the vote on equal terms with men.

**1929** Margaret Bondfield becomes the first British woman cabinet minister.

**1936** In France three women are appointed to the government eight years before French women get the vote in 1944.

**1945** The end of the Second World War sees women's suffrage introduced in Albania, Hungary, Italy, Japan and Yugoslavia.

Getting the vote does not result in the immediate implementation of other social and legal reforms which earlier campaigners had hoped for.

In France, for example, the principle of equal pay for equal work is drafted in 1946, but it is not until 1982 that the necessary government legislation against sex discrimination in employment, pay and career prospects is drawn up.

**1968** The National Organization for Women, founded by Betty Friedan in the USA, provides the impetus for the rebirth of the feminist movement and a new round of legislation on women's rights.

**1970** The Equal Pay Act is passed in Britain saying that a woman must be paid the same rate as a man for the same, or broadly similar, work. It is not fully implemented till 1975.

**1971** Women in Switzerland get the vote and ten years later the Swiss constitution is amended to give women equal rights. In one of the Swiss cantons women still cannot vote on regional issues.

**1975** The Sex Discrimination Act in Britain makes it unlawful to treat a woman less favourably than a man in the same circumstances.

**1975** Equal Opportunity Commission is set up to monitor the working of the Sex Discrimination and Equal Pay Acts.

**1984** Liechtenstein is the last European country to give women the right to vote.

*A woman in the White House? Geraldine Ferraro is chosen to attract the female vote, 1984.*

# How to find out more

### General
The best place to start is with your **local library**. Not only will the Librarian be able to help you browse among the shelves for books on women, but they will also have addresses of local organizations that might be of use. Local history societies might help or you might find a Women's Studies Course at a local college of education.

For information about women in specific countries try the relevant **embassies**. These are mostly in London.

Many areas will have **women's organizations** for different ethnic groups. The following organizations have their national headquarters in London and will put you in touch with local groups:

Bangladeshi Women's Association, 91 Highbury Hill, London N5

UK Asian Women's Conference, 19 Wykeham Road, London NW4

West Indian Women's Association, 71 Pound Lane, Willesden, London NW10

### Resource centres
Equal Opportunities Commission, Overseas House, Quay Street, Manchester M3 3HW (061 833 9244)
Set up in 1975 to monitor the Sex Discrimination Act, it has an information centre and library as well as being the body to whom you take any complaints about discrimination.

Fawcett Library, City of London Polytechnic, Calcutta House, Old Castle Street, London E1 7NT
Britain's main centre for books on feminism and women in general. The bulk of the material concerns women in Britain but there is also a great deal of material from the USA and the Commonwealth.
(The Fawcett Library charges a small subscription fee.)

Feminist Library and Information Centre, Hungerford House, Victoria Embankment, London WC2 (01-930 0715)
Has a large collection of material on women's history and information about academic courses on women's studies. Also at Hungerford House is 'A Women Place' with a café and bookshop and more general information about women in London.

Women's Information and Referral Service (WIRES), PO Box 162, Sheffield 11UD (0742 755290)
Provides information about current campaigns, and all aspects of the women's movement. Produces a national newsletter which comes out every three months.

CREW, Centre for Research on European Women, 22 Rue de Toulouse, 1040 Brussels, Belgium (010 32 2640 45 16)
Monitors the role and treatment of women in EEC countries.

National Council for Civil Liberties, 21 Tabard Street, London SE1 (01-403 3888)
Publishes a great variety of books and pamphlets which include practical guides on women's rights, and surveys on discrimination in education and at work.

Rights of Women, 377 Gray's Inn Road, London WC1
A collective group of lawyers specializing in the law and how it affects women. They also run a 'Help line'.

Federation of Worker Writers and Community Publishers, 45 Gelston Point, Burwell Close, London E1 2NR
Their publications list includes a lot of working-class autobiographies – many of them written by women and very easy (and fascinating) to read.

Office of Population Census and Surveys, St Catherine's House, 10 Kingsway, London WC2
Keep statistics on virtually everything from divorce rates to women in the labour force. Have published a survey on women and employment.

The Age Exchange Theatre, 15 Camden Row, Blackheath, London SE3
Much of their work is based on oral history (including a project about women working during the war which has a book to go with it).

Women and Development Unit, Commonwealth Secretariat, Quadrant House, Pall Mall, London SW1
Acts as a focal point for the needs of women in the Commonwealth.

National Association of Youth Clubs, Girls Work, 30 Peacock Lane, Leicester LE1 5NY (0533 29514)
Provide information for girls on a wide variety of topics including work. Produce a newsletter.

# Reading list

**General**

Anna Pollert, *Girls, Wives, Factory Lives* (Macmillan, 1981)
A book about women workers, about the work they do and the way they feel about it. Based on interviews with women workers at the Churchman Tobacco Factory in Bristol and packed with quotations from them.

Anna Coote and Beatrix Campbell, *Sweet Freedom: The Struggle for Women's Liberation* (Picador, 1982)
A look at the progress of women's liberation so far and the reasons for its achievements and failures. Draws together much useful information; a comprehensive index makes the information required easy to look up.

Deirdre Sanders with Jane Read, *Kitchen Sink or Swim: Women in the 80s* (Penguin, 1982)
A look at what is happening to the position of women in the 80s. Again, is packed with quotations with a useful index.

Mary Langham, *Now We Are 30: Women of the Breakthrough Generation* (Eyre Methuen, 1981)
An account of the progress of women born in the late '40s, the 'bulge' generation, based on interviews with the author's schoolfriends. A good general account of the '50s, '60s and '70s, and the role of women and the growth of the women's movement during this period.

Carol Adams and Rae Lavrikietis, *The Gender Trap* (Quartet, 1980)
Well set out and easy to read. Looks at sex discrimination in different areas.

Shere Hite, *The Hite Report* (Summit, 1977)
An investigation of women's sexuality based on questionnaires sent out to women.

Anna Coote and Tess Gill, *Women's Rights: A Practical Guide* (Penguin)
A classic textbook.

Joyce Nicholson, *What Society Does to Girls* (Virago, 1980)
Looks at how girls are conditioned. Written for young people.

Angela Phillips and Jill Rakusen (eds), *Our Bodies Ourselves: A Health Book by and for Women* (Penguin, 1978)
A handbook on women's health with clear factual information on a wide range of topics.

Kaleghl Quinn, *Stand Your Ground* (Orbis, 1983)
A self-defence manual.

*In the Pink: The Raging Beauties. Poems from the show and many more* (Women's Press, 1984)
Poems by women, some funny, some angry.

Greta Kent, *A View from the Bandstand* (Sheba Press, 1983)
Photo collection from the family albums of a woman who worked with 'Ladies' Orchestras' at the turn of the century.

Ann Oakley, *Subject Women* (Fontana, 1981)
An analysis of women's situation today with masses of useful statistical information.

**Women's history**

Deirdre Beddoe, *Discovering Women's History, A Practical Manual* (Pandora Press, 1983)
A guide for people who want to find out about the lives of women in the past.

Sheila Rowbotham, *Hidden From History* (Pluto, 1973)
A study of the changing position of women.

Carol Adams, *Ordinary Lives: A Hundred Years Ago* (Virago, 1982)
Looks at the changes in the everyday experiences of ordinary people. Easy to read.

Margaret Llewellyn Davies (ed.), *Maternity: Letters from Working Women* (Virago, 1978)
Margaret Llewellyn Davies (ed.), *Cooperative Working Women: Life as We Have Known It* (Virago, 1977)
A first-hand record of the lives, experiences and aspirations of working women whose recollections go back to the 1850s.

Jill Liddington and Jill Norris, *One Hand Tied Behind Us* (Virago, 1978)
An account of the struggle for the vote by working women in the north of England.

Maud Pember Reeves (ed.) *Round About a Pound a Week* (Virago, 1978)
An account of poor women's lives before the First World War.

Dale Spender, *There's Always been a Women's Movement This Century* (Pandora Press, 1983)
Interviews with Dora Russell, Hazel Hunkins Halliman, Mary Stott, Constance Rover and Rebecca West.

*Making History 2: Women* (TV History Centre, 1983)
Pamphlet on recording women's history available from Television History Centre, 42 Queen Square, London WC1N 3AJ.

Margery Spring Rice, *Working Class Wives* (Virago, 1981)
About women in the 1930s.

Mary Lee Settle, *All the Brave Promises* (Pandora Press, 1984)
Autobiography of WAAF women in the Second World War.

**Interviews with women**
Carola Hanssan and Karin Liden, *Moscow Women: 13 interviews* (Allison and Busby, 1984)
Based on interviews with women in Moscow but also giving background information about the woman's role in the Soviet Union.

Jean McCrindle and Sheila Rowbotham (eds.), *Dutiful Daughters* (Penguin, 1983)
Women talk about their lives. Fascinating and usually down to earth.

Ann Oakley, *From Here to Maternity* (Pelican, 1981)
Interviews with 60 women about what it is *really* like having a baby.

Ann Oakley, *Housewife* (Pelican, 1976)
Traces the historical development of the housewife role and the present day situation of women as housewives, illustrated by four case histories. Interviews particularly interesting.

Sue Sharpe, *'Just Like a Girl'* (Penguin, 1976)
How girls learn to be women. Based on interviews with Ealing schoolgirls. Large sections in their own words.

**Women in politics**
Barbara Rogers, *52%: Getting Women's Power Into Politics* (Women's Press, 1983)

Elizabeth Vallance, *Women in the House* (Athlone Press, 1979)

Amrit Wilson, *Finding A Vote: Asian Women in Britain* (Virago, 1978)

Dorothy Thompson (ed.) *Over Our Dead Bodies – Women Against the Bomb* (Virago, 1983)

**Publishers**
Virago Press, 41 William IV Street, London WC2N 4DB

The Women's Press, 124 Shoreditch High Street, London E1

These two publishers specialize in books by and about women. Look out for their books in the bookshop or library, or browse through their catalogues for further information and ideas.

The Feminist Book Fair Group has published a useful catalogue, *259, An Introduction to a World of Women's Books*, which looks at publishing all over the world and provides a checklist of titles.

# Film and video

There are film and video workshops run for and by women in various parts of the country. They will provide tapes they have made, and in some cases help to train women in the use of video.

Cinema of Women, 27 Clerkenwell Close, London EC1R 0AT
Distributes films by and about women.

Barefoot Video, 50 Brunswick Street, West Hove, Sussex BN2 1EZ

Sheffield Film Co-Op, Albreda House, Lydgate Lane, Sheffield S10 5FH

Women in Sync, Room 1/2, 38 Mount Pleasant, London WC1.

Independent Film and Video Association, Women's Film and Television Network, 79 Wardour Street, London W1
Should be able to put you in touch with film and video groups in your area.

# Index

Numbers in **bold** refer to illustrations and captions.

advertising 6, 11, 52
Albania 58
alimony 44
arranged marriages 42
Astor, Nancy 59
Athens 4
Austen, Jane 27
Australia 32, 35
Austria 58

Baader-Meinhof 48
Babylonia 4
Bandaranaike, Sirimavo 24
Beeton, Mrs 40
Beveridge Report 13
Bonaparte, Napoleon 32
Bondfield, Margaret 59
Bonsor, Sir Nicholas 36
Boy George **53**
Britain 24, 27, 28, 31, 32, 34, 44
Brontë Sisters 26
Bundestag 25
Burgess, Anthony 27

Campaign for Nuclear Disarmament 25
Canada 24, 32, 34, 58
Cartland, Barbara 27, 47
Chandler, Raymond 27
chauvinism 22
Chesser, Dr Eustace 50
Chesterfield, Lord 50
childcare facilities 14, 39
China **5**
Christie, Agatha 27
contraceptive pill 13
creativity 26-7
Czechoslovakia 58

Dally, Dr Ann 37
Davidson, Emily 58
delinquents 14
depression 54
Dickens, Charles 27
divorce 40, 41, 44

education 27, 28, 31
Egypt 4
Eliot, George 27
equal opportunities 56
Equal Opportunities Commission 31, 59, 60
equal pay 13, 35, 56
Equal Pay Act 59
equal rights 56

fairy tales 9
family life 32, 38, 39
father 37, 44, 45
female infanticide 5
feminism 56
Ferraro, Geraldine **59**
fifties, the 12
Finland 24, 58
Forsyth, Frederick 27
France 24, 25, 32, 33
Friedan, Betty 59

gentleness 48, **49**
Germany, East 32
Germany, West 32
Gandhi, Indira 24
Goethe 26
Greenham Common 25, 56

Hodgson, Dr 28
House of Commons 25
housework 16, 17, 18
    wages for 16
Hungary 58

India 5
Ingham, Mary 44
Israel 39, 48
Italians 4
Italy 58

Japan 58
Jenkin, Patrick 15

Kelly, Petra 25
Kenny, Mary 56
kibbutz **38**

Lessing, Doris 27
London Transport 20
love 9

managers 22
marriage 40, 41, 42, 43
Markiewicz, Constance 59
medicine 27
Meir, Golda 24
Middle Ages 4
Miss World **7**
Mohammed, Prophet 4
money 24, 35
Moscow **20**
mother 6, 37

National Organization for Women 58
National Union of Women's Suffrage Societies 58
Netherlands 58
New Zealand 31, 35
nursery rhymes 9

Oakley, Ann 19

Old Testament 7

Palestine 48
Petrarch 4
Picasso 26
pin money 14
Poland 58
politics 24, 25
pop music 10, 11
positive discrimination 21
pregnancy 47
publishing 27

Rowbotham, Sheila 12

salaries 20
Sand, George 27
science **26**, 27
Senate, US 25
sex 46
sex discrimination 13, 56
sex roles 9, 10, 21
sexism 56
Shakespeare 26
Shaw, George Bernard 43
single-parent families 38
sixties, the 12, 13
South America 48
Spock, Dr
*Sunday Times* 47
Sweden 24
Switzerland 59

taxation 35
Thackeray, William 27
Thatcher, Margaret 24, 25, 26
tomboys 9
TUC 20

Ullmann, Liv 5
unemployment 13, 14, 42
university 31
USA 14, 21, 24, 44
USSR 14, 58

Vietcong 48
Victorian 51

Wollstonecraft, Mary 28, 58
woman priest **21**
women's liberation 4, 13, 56
women's suffrage 56
work 14, 15, 18, 20, 21, 32, 54
working mothers 14
Wyoming 58

Yugoslavia 58

# Credits

The author and publishers would like to thank Penguin Books for permission to quote extracts from *Just Like a Girl* by Sue Sharpe (interviews with schoolgirls); and Macmillan for permission to quote extracts from *Girls, Wives, Factory Lives* by Anna Pollert (interviews with factory workers).

Thanks are also due to the following for kind permission to reproduce copyright illustrations:

Aldus Archive: 52
Associated Press: 59
Barnaby's Picture Library: 12, 13, 58
Earthscan/Mark Edwards: 34-35
Family Planning Association: 47
Francis Fashesin: 8
Format/
   Pam Isherwood: 24
   Jenny Matthews: 6, 36
   Maggie Murray: 20
   Raissa Page: 5, 15, 43
   Brenda Prince: 16, 19, 55, 57
   Val Wilmer: 26
Richard and Sally Greenhill: cover, 17, 18-19, 28-29, 30, 38, 39, 45, 49
Mansell Collection: 4, 33
Popperfoto: 46
Rex Features: 7, 10-11, 23, 25, 48, 50-51, 53
David Richardson: 40-41, 42

Picture research by Caroline Mitchell.
Design by Norman Reynolds.